Also by the Nosh Brothers

ENTERTAINING
published by Macmillan

WINTER NOSH

THE NOSH BROTHERS

Indulgence

PHOTOGRAPHY BY KELVIN MURRAY

MACMILLAN

First published 1998 by Macmillan

an imprint of Macmillan Publishers Ltd
25 Eccleston Place, London SW1W 9NF
and Basingstoke

Associated companies throughout the world

ISBN 0 333 74108 0

1 3 5 7 9 8 6 4 2

A CIP catalogue record for this book in available from
the British Library.

Typeset by Florencetype Ltd, Stoodleigh, Devon
Printed and bound in Great Britain by
The Bath Press Ltd

Contents

The Ultimate Breakfast

Simply Indulgent

Cheese-of-all-Cheeses 41

French Beans with Roast Garlic 42

Chilli Aïoli 43

Home-made Crisps 44

Fresh Oysters with Shallot Vinegar and Jalapeño
Pepper Sauce 46

Start as You Mean to Go On
48

Marinated Chargrilled Baby Octopus
on Rocket Salad 51

Fresh Figs Baked in Parma Ham with
a Fresh Raspberry Vinaigrette 52

Chargrilled Carpaccio of Beef Fillet
with Infused Lemon Oil, Black Pepper and
Shaved Parmesan 54

Smoked Mussel Pâté with Brioche Melba Toasts 55

Champagne and Camembert Soup
with Onion Croutons 56

Fettucine Alfredo 58

Roasted Elephant Garlic with
Tomato and Rosemary Ciabatta 62

White Asparagus with a Warm
Hollandaise, Shallots and Pancetta 62

King Neptune's Gazpacho 64

Basil Gnocchi with Gorgonzola,
White Wine and Parmesan 65

Elegant Sufficiencies
68

Mains for all Seasons
80

Contents

7

Indian Feast

Marinated King Prawns with Tomato, Chargrilled Chilli and Coriander Salsa 97

Nosh Stuffed Naan 98

Mint and Cucumber Raita 100

'Emperor' Chicken Tikka Curry with Almonds and Basmati Rice 101

Spiced Lemon Dhal 103

Japanese Feast

Tuna 'Kobe' Carpaccio with Soy Sauce, Ginger, Wasabe and Virgin Olive Oil 106

Swordfish on a Bed of Samphire 106

Crispy Duck 'Hiroshima' with Spinach and Sesame Seeds 108

Vegetable Tempura with Garlic Soy Sauce Dip 109

Sesame and Ginger Dipping Sauce 111

Spicy Seafood and Chicken Ramen 112

Deep-fried King Prawns with Sweet Chilli Jam and Limes 114

Contents

Sweetly Indulgent

140

Baklava and Turkish Coffee 142

Peach Ice Cream with Bourbon 145

Armagnac Prunes with Sauternes
Caramel Creams 146

Brandied Apricot Filos with Powdered
Crystallized Orange 148

Hot Raspberry Soufflé 149

Nosh Pecan Fudge Brownies with White
Chocolate and Sambuca Sauce 150

Vanilla Ice Cream Baked in
Meringue, with a Warm
Mocha Sabayon Sauce 153

Coconut and Water Chestnut Custard 154

Panettone Pudding with Cognac 155

Raspberry Ice Cream with Cassis 156

Mango Kulfi 158

Down the Hatch

160

Nosh Bloody Moses 162

Sweet Lassi with Pistachios 164

Iced Kahlua Coffee 134

Bollinger RD with Chilled Wild
Strawberries 165

Gimlets 167

Contents

11

Indulgence

12

'The taking of one's pleasure freely'

Indulgence is all about being a bit selfish. It's not about being overtly self-indulgent but more about giving yourself and your friends a treat to elevate your enjoyment of those simple pleasures in life. What could be more fundamental to life than food? We look at getting the best out of some of the simplest ingredients as well as a few really special things. But remember, not everything we suggest need cost the earth – even if the results are lavish. The Nosh Brothers are interested in getting you the maximum pleasure out of eating. This could be from something as straightforward as a sandwich made with no added complications other than simply baking your own bread to achieve top results. Don't be shy, though, to eat a superb dish on your own – indulging yourself is not a sin! So, to enjoy your meal to the full, we think you should devote plenty of time to the atmosphere of the eating ceremony and treat the whole affair with due reverence – this will ensure that all who partake in the feast are fulfilled.

The Nosh Brothers' cuisine is synonymous with eating in style – at whatever level, so *Indulgence* is a logical progression for us. When we were writing our first book, *Entertaining*, we chose to put the accent on creating an achievable but impressive standard for dinner parties, meals to prepare for your friends at home that would not look out of place in a decent restaurant. *Indulgence*, on the other hand, is a celebration of food in its own right. Not content with simply strolling through the further reaches of our kitchen repertoire, we would ask you to join us as we scale the summit of culinary luxury.

Appreciation of all things gourmet has too often been associated with a select few – the domain of an almost Masonic elite of rich people, old-school-tie wine traders, crusty food critics and the like. We feel this is deeply unfair. It leaves ordinary people ostracized simply for their lack of snobbery, and unable to join in the fantastic new waves of food trends lapping around the world.

So the Nosh Brothers present to you *Indulgence*. Although it's written for everyone, we still hope it will introduce you to the very best of new tastes. Think of it not so much as a road map to the best in a supermarket, but as a treasure map to the culinary riches that can be discovered in your own kitchen.

Nosh Style

The Nosh Brothers, as Britain's most irreverent chefs, have, via our radio and television shows, and their own restaurant ventures, long been associated with the vanguard of a new movement in cooking which has overturned the dainty food rules of the 1980s and helped to establish a new robust style – demystifying and demolishing the traditions associated with the arrogances and mysteries hanging over from a world obsession with classic French cuisine.

The last few years have produced a wide and dynamic range of influences from far beyond our shores: the Pacific Rim, the Mediterranean and most of south-east Asia. These influences have blended into a 'fusion', which is a food term in its own right, as well as informing what the food press term 'Modern British' cuisine. Our intention has been not only to synthesize these influences but to give them a twist of our own – producing what might be called 'Modern International'. Thus has evolved our own enlightened method of cooking with an attitude, the Nosh Style, a 'Full-on Formula' that can embrace both the simplest fare and the most royal.

The Recipes, Ingredients, and Presentation

It is safe for you to assume that most dishes presented in this book will have a degree of lavishness attached. Not for the sake of being 'flash', you understand, rather for a sense of quiet, understated luxury. No overly adorned chicken breasts here (we've seen them tarted up in gold leaf) – rather the simple principle that there is more luxury and taste in a simple baked potato with soured cream and Beluga caviar than any attempt at nouvelle nonsense!

Dishes are presented as follows: The Ultimate Breakfast; Simply Indulgent (simple items that are quick and easy to prepare); Begin As You Mean to Go On (starters); Elegant Sufficiencies (substantially filling dishes that can either be presented as a starter or if made slightly larger will be ideal as a main dish eaten alone); Mains For All Seasons, A World of Indulgence (feasts from around the world); Sweetly Indulgent (desserts); and Down the Hatch – which, as drinks, are self-explanatory.

Since the accent is on the degree of luxury associated with a particular recipe, the produce and other ingredients used should all be of the lushest quality. It is important to note that unlike some 'cheffy' books, the dishes are all achievable in a real sense; any overly grandiose methods have been removed in favour of easy-to-cook Nosh shortcuts that do not compromise on taste.

In general, the ingredients can be sourced without resorting to obscure suppliers. However, it's always wise to familiarize yourself with your local specialist food shops and delis. They often have good supplies of the rarer ingredients, and shopping with a quality local supplier is often a refreshing contrast to a supermarket.

All the little extras are important to get right, from laying the table to the temperature you serve the dish at. Taking time and care over this is an important signal to any guests to join in with the spirit of the event. A tip worth remembering is always cook something that you feel confident with and happy to attempt – only try a dummy run on people you don't like very much then if you make a pig's ear of it and your so-called friends don't talk to you again, so what, you've lost nothing!

Indulgence is intended as an indispensable, ultimate guide for all bon viveurs who want a different slant on their cooking – and thereby the Nosh fast track to raising their standard of living.

CHOLLA FRENCH TOAST,
DREDGED WITH CINNAMON SUGAR
WITH CRISPY BACON AND MAPLE SYRUP

'LASAGNE' OF SMOKED SALMON
AND SCRAMBLED EGG WITH KETA

SMOKED HADDOCK AND CHEESE SOUFFLÉ

CROISSANTS WITH GRUYÈRE
AND SMOKED HAM

PERFECT COFFEE

The Ultimate Breakfast

It all starts with the alarm clock (or a radio DJ droning on chirpily about nothing in particular – whatever works for you). Then, after a number of jabs at the snooze button, it's tea, coffee, or a painkiller – you choose the brand. But next comes the most hit-and-miss part of regaining consciousness: breakfast. Kellogg's have wonderful offerings from low fat to high fibre – and all stops in between – but for a fully-loaded treat, some effort is required.

Breakfast is to most people a bit of a luxury, as there's always something in the morning that seems more important – work, an extra five minutes under the duvet or a quick shag. But if you do manage to get up and feel in the mood for a super upmarket breakfast, these are a few dishes we highly recommend. Hey, it might become a habit.

In many ways, breakfast is still our favourite meal. It was, historically, the most important meal of the day for working people, but is much less so these days, and the traditional choices of morning cooked food have also dwindled. Sadly, modern eating habits have relegated the traditional English Breakfast to the transport café or a hotel treat. A Continental holiday breakfast of feta cheese and olives has its novelty, but True Brits pine for some decent grub after only a couple of days. If British hearts are made of oak then a full English breakfast is the stuff our arms and legs are made of.

The British Way of Life has at its heart bacon and eggs. Medicos and health pundits now wag their fingers disapprovingly, telling us how bad all that saturated fat is for us. Yet our taste buds don't absorb such propaganda – who can resist the aroma of bacon frying first thing in the morning? Not us! Many of us smuggle bacon to Muslim countries to ensure a good start to the day, so keep the flag flying and if you spot us at customs with a smile on our faces and suspiciously bulky suits, keep *schtumm* . . . you'll know. Whether you poach, fry, boil or scramble, egg freshness is *de rigueur*. Date stamps and free-range hens all help to elevate the humble ovoid to gourmet status. (Eggshell is porous and will let in air in time, so check the date stamp carefully.) It is worth noting that the fashion for buying jumbo eggs is ill advised. Generally, big eggs come from big birds (i.e., old birds), with smaller-sized from smaller (younger) birds, so maximize your flavour by using 5 small eggs for your omelette instead of 3 large.

Who hasn't despaired at the sight of your vac-packed rashers shrinking in the pan, leaving behind a white scummy deposit? This is the result of deep-saline injection in the factory, producing fast-cure bacon cheaply for the mass-market . . . not a pretty sight. Quality bacon should be dry cured, which draws the meat juices out slowly, resulting in a firmer, less salty bacon that doesn't shrink.

When choosing sausages get a brand that has a high proportion of non-fat meat. A degree of fat is needed to grill to a good result, but don't buy anything with an 'economy' tag to it. It will be full of filler and tallow and taste like fried carpet. Traditionally made black pudding is fine, but usually it's simply gash offal indifferently squeezed into a sock by heartless butchers keen to rid themselves of spare pet food.

Forced Dutch and Spanish salad tomatoes don't add much to the breakfast but decent beefsteak tomatoes can be OK. A pinch of Italian herbs helps to boost flavour but purists would be scornful of this as an affectation straying into Nancy-boy Potter territory.

Closed cap or flat field mushrooms? The debate continues. Copious amounts of black liquor from flatties spoils the appearance of the dish but if you don't give a damn then field mushrooms are your thing. (However, if your closed caps are a little bland, zap them up with a splash of soy sauce and lemon juice.)

While still number one fans of the good old British fry-up it is our duty to elevate and evolve the breakfast to its rightful place in kitchen status, so we have prepared for you a selection of some fine ideas on a cooked theme that really cut the mustard!

Cholla French toast, dredged with cinnamon sugar with crispy bacon and maple syrup

SERVES 2

On our last visit to New York we intended to research various food ideas, eyeball some media tycoons with television interests and get some serious eating and drinking done. From cocktails at the Plaza to some seriously fashionable restaurants we ate and drank in grand style. Apart from one slightly suspect sandwich bar in midtown the fare was memorable, particularly the offerings from the humble diner. On almost any main street you can find a typical diner churning out mighty breakfasts from an early hour that put the average British 'greasy spoon' café to shame. Immaculately clean, they serve anything from toast and filled bagels to fruit muffins and full cooked breakfasts.

On our last morning, we witnessed a giant of a man (who would dwarf the two of us!), sitting on a tubular steel chair which he overflowed by a generous amount, ordering his breakfast in a broad Brooklyn accent: 'I wan' a three-egg omelette, whites only, with onions, and I wan' the onions burnt – with toast, white, buttered in the kitchen, not on the plate, without any of that friggin' grape jelly, an' a coffee, white, no sugar, with skimmed milk . . .' and so it went on. In England his brusque manner would have been interpreted as rudeness and he would probably have been asked to leave. As it was, he was simply being assertive, knew what he wanted and the waitress brought it for him. And she got a $5 tip for a $12 meal – so the system works!

Our memorable dish from this encounter, fondly remembered and reproduced here for you was a light piece of French toast, made with cholla, the Jewish milk bread, lightly fried in an eggy batter and served with a dusting of icing sugar and some crispy streaky bacon (indeed, it is hard to find bacon in New York cooked and presented any other way). With a couple of spoonfuls of rich maple syrup it is a satisfying and luxurious start to the day.

4 rashers dry-cure smoked streaky bacon
4 tbsp whole milk
2 eggs
a pinch each of Maldon sea salt and freshly
    ground black pepper
4 slices cholla milk bread, thickly sliced
6 tbsp sunflower oil
60g unsalted butter

TO SERVE
equal parts icing sugar and cinnamon, mixed
maple syrup

Method

Set the grill on a high heat. Remove the rind from the rashers, stretch each one with the blade of a kitchen knife and snip the fat with scissors every 5mm to help prevent the bacon curling and twisting. Grill the rashers until crisp.

Whisk the milk with the eggs and season with salt and pepper. Pour onto a plate and soak each slice of cholla thoroughly in it. Put a large frying pan on a medium flame and heat up half the oil with half the butter until hot but not smoking. Reduce the flame to low and slowly fry two slices of the eggy bread until light golden-brown.

You should aim to cook the bread so that the inside is not soggy but without burning or crisping the outside too early. About 3–4 minutes each side should be enough, depending on the thickness and freshness of the bread. When cooked throughout, drain on kitchen paper, keep warm, and wipe the pan out. Replenish with a fresh complement of oil and butter (this prevents any burning of butter residues and gives a clean-looking result) and repeat for the other two slices. When they have all been cooked, dust the top surfaces lightly with the icing sugar and cinnamon.

Serve with the grilled crispy rashers and a generous pouring of maple syrup.

'Lasagne' of smoked salmon and scrambled egg with keta

SERVES 2

This is not only one of the loveliest dishes that could ever greet the eye first thing, pleasures of the flesh notwithstanding, but it is a rare instance of something with a great element of sophistication and style that's chock-full of flavour too. A rich yet delicate little number, so don't overdo it or there will be no room for lunch!

Most people's scrambled egg is cooked perfectly at the time it comes out of the pan. But as it's delivered to the table it cooks on, congeals and spoils. There are two ways out of this: to eat out of the pan at the stove, which isn't very sociable, or to stir in a cupful of single cream, which keeps it nice and moist with a small-grained texture.

60g unsalted butter
4 small free-range eggs
salt and freshly ground white pepper
2 tbsp single cream
4 slices buttered white toast trimmed into
*   7cm × 10cm rectangles*

a little cream cheese
*10 slices smoked salmon, cut to fit the toast**
90g soured cream
small jar keta (salmon caviar)

TO SERVE
freshly ground black pepper

Scrambled egg method

Put a heavy-based frying pan over a low to medium heat, and melt the butter in it. Whisk the eggs gently, using a fork to keep the yolk and white textures from becoming too homogenized, and season with the salt and pepper. Pour the mixture into the pan, keep stirring with a wooden spoon, and agitate gently until nearly set. Then add the single cream and stir in, removing from the heat immediately.

Assembly method

Warm plates and toast should be ready. Spread some cream cheese on the toast (to stop it going soggy), then spoon some of the egg mixture on top. Add a slice of smoked salmon, then spread another thin layer of scrambled egg on top. Continue making thin alternating layers of salmon and egg until you've built up a stack, resembling lasagne.

For topping off, finish with a layer of salmon and using a palette knife, spread a thin layer of soured cream over the stack, then sprinkle liberally with keta. This mimics the white sauce and grated topping of lasagne. This smoked salmon 'lasagne' should be finished with a grinding of black pepper and served immediately.

* Smoked salmon varies in quality from oily and salty to a rich dense-textured flesh with a distinct smoky taste. Traditionally, Isle of Skye salmon has a fine reputation but there are many small smokeries that produce excellent results. It is a matter of testing and trying by trial and error, to find one that suits your palate. Ironically, although wild salmon makes well-flavoured dishes, the lesser fat content than farmed salmon means that it doesn't take on the smoke so deeply.

Smoked haddock and cheese soufflé

SERVES 2

Soufflés always seemed to be a perfect supper dish until a Swedish friend served one up for breakfast during a skiing trip in the Arctic Circle. We had no bread or rolls, but plenty of eggs and smoked fish supplied from a nearby farm. To us, soufflés had always appeared to be a kind of cooking that would have eluded cooks such as ourselves who assiduously avoided professional training, and soufflé style positively reeked of 1960s dinner parties, to be served along with quiche and pineapple and cheese on sticks. We had never bothered with them – until that fateful holiday.

In the Arctic Circle night-time can be very bright when you experience the Midnight Sun (in the polar region the sun never quite sets in the summer). Conveniently, this blurs the time difference between supper and breakfast. It may as well always be breakfast time! So this soufflé is quite appropriate for an avant-ski breakfast when you want something other than bacon and eggs or toast.

1 tbsp unsalted butter, melted
1 tbsp fresh white breadcrumbs
90g smoked haddock fillet
150ml whole milk
2 bay leaves
1 small onion, peeled and roughly chopped
8 black peppercorns
30g unsalted butter
30g plain flour
a pinch of English mustard powder
Maldon sea salt
a pinch of cayenne pepper
5 small eggs, separated
60g Gruyère cheese, finely grated
freshly ground black pepper

Method

Preheat the oven to 200°C/400°F/gas mark 6. Brush a 15cm soufflé dish with the melted butter and sprinkle the breadcrumbs evenly around the base and side.

Put the fish in the milk in a flat pan with the bay leaves, onion and peppercorns, cover the pan with foil, and poach in the oven for 10–15 minutes. Strain the milk and reserve. When the haddock is cool, flake with a fork into medium-sized pieces and reserve. Discard any skin and bones.

Next, make a roux in a saucepan with the butter and flour, then add the mustard powder and stir for about 1 minute. Season with salt and cayenne pepper. Add the fish milk and stir well to make a thick sauce. Ensure that all the lumps are removed (use a balloon whisk if necessary).

Allow the sauce to cool slightly. Whisk the egg whites until stiff, then beat the egg yolks and fold into the béchamel with the flaked haddock and cheese. Mix half of the whites into the sauce/yolk/fish mix and combine well, seasoning with freshly ground black pepper. Then fold the remaining whites lightly into the mixture.

Spoon the soufflé mixture into the dish, which should ideally be not more than two-thirds full. Bake for 20–25 minutes, during which time the mixture will rise to above the top of the dish. To ensure a smooth rise, do not open the oven door until at least 15 minutes into the cooking time (a glass-fronted oven door is useful here). Just poke the dish with an oven glove through the slightly open door to see if the soufflé wobbles. If after 20 minutes it seems too slack, cook on for another 5 minutes. Serve immediately.

Croissants with Gruyère and smoked ham

SERVES 4: MAKES ABOUT 16 CROISSANTS

Croissants are fiddly to make, but well worth the effort. There is a world of difference between the cotton wool efforts found in cellophane on supermarket shelves and the buttery crisp flavour of a real fresh-baked croissant.

The flaky buttery roll we all know and love (translating literally as 'crescent' – in recognition of the symbolic Islamic sickle moon) was introduced into Central and Western Europe from the Middle East via invasions of the Ottomans, with their Turkish and Persian bakers in tow. It found a home in the Viennese patisserie and then caught on eastwards in France, and eventually, in the latter half of the twentieth century, Britain.

Croissants, once baked, can be reheated

without losing much texture or flavour, but don't last much beyond twenty-four hours as they dry out rapidly. We recommend making a quantity of dough, using what you need now and freezing the remainder for another rising and baking session. By using one of the new-type quick-acting dried yeasts you can save time on all the traditional mixing, 'brewing' and waiting around involved with a fresh yeast.

Croissants make a perfect breakfast on their own, accompanied by a good dollop of strawberry or raspberry jam, but here is a good savoury idea for a more substantial start to the day – stuffed with Gruyère cheese and thinly sliced smoked ham.

500g strong white bread flour
60g caster sugar
10g fine Maldon sea salt
2 sachets quick-acting dried yeast
30g dried milk powder
340ml cold water
240g unsalted butter

TO SERVE
8 thin slices of mature Gruyère cheese (not
 the cheap waxy stuff)
8 medium-cut slices of Westphalian smoked ham

Croissant method

The dough must be prepared the day before baking.

Place the flour, sugar, salt, yeast and milk powder in the bowl of an electric mixer. Use a bread-dough hook attachment, and add the water slowly until the dough comes away from the side of the bowl. Next, cover the dough with a damp tea towel and leave to rise in a warm place (25–30°C/75–86°F) for 45–60 minutes. It should double in volume.

Next, briefly flip the dough over to release the gases – this is called 'knocking back'. Now shape it into a rectangular slab and put it back in the bowl. Cover it with clingfilm, and place in the fridge for 6–8 hours or overnight.

The next process is to work the butter into the dough alternately folding and rolling to double over the slab of dough, incorporating the butter into layers which will eventually give the pastry its distinctive flaky nature.

Place the rectangle of dough on a floured rolling surface and roll out the four sides into 'ears' or 'flaps'. Have the butter at the same temperature as the dough, and place it in the middle. Now fold the four flaps over the butter, making an envelope that completely covers the butter, then flour the dough and roll it into a 40 × 60cm rectangle. Fold it into four, wrap again in clingfilm and chill in the freezer compartment for 10 minutes.

Roll it out to a 40 × 60cm rectangle again and repeat the rolling process, but folding in the opposite direction. Then wrap and chill again for 10 minutes. Then repeat the folding/rolling process twice more.

Now roll out the dough on a floured surface to about 40 × 75cm, which will give a thickness of about 2–3mm. To ensure you cut accurate triangular croissant shapes every time, make a cardboard template in the shape of an isosceles triangle measuring 15 × 15 × 18cm:

Mark out your triangles by laying the short edge of the template along the long edge of the pastry sheet and draw the outline of the shape with the back of a knife. Now flip the cardboard over and mark another shape next to it. Continue along the line of pastry until you have at least 16 or so shapes – then cut them out completely into neat-edged triangles.

Set the triangles on a floured surface and roll the shape up from the long point nearest you into a cylinder; twist the two points around into a curved horn or crescent shape, pinching the points together where they meet. Place on a tray, arranged so that the edges of the croissants do not touch.

Brush with beaten egg and leave to rise in a warm, humid place (25–30°C/75–85°F) for 2 hours or so or until they have doubled in size. Finally, before baking in a hot oven (230°C/450°F/gas mark 8), brush once more with beaten egg. About 15 minutes should be plenty.

Cool on a wire rack. To reheat, simply place in a warm oven (160°C/325°F/gas mark 3) for 3–4 minutes. If cooking straight from the freezer, place the frozen croissants into a very hot oven (250°C/475°F/gas mark 9) for 5–6 minutes. As before, cool on a wire rack.

Assembly

Use 8 large croissants, cut across the back, horizontally. Place a slice each of cheese and ham in each croissant and warm them through in a medium oven (190°C/375°F/gas mark 5) until heated through – and then serve immediately.

This assembly is the simplest method in the book – but don't underestimate the problems entailed by operating with a hangover!

Perfect Coffee

It's worth getting coffee right. While most people can make a reasonable cup with whatever method they prefer, we feel that in the main there's still a long way to go as far as preparation goes.

First, start with your bean. It needs to be good quality and well roasted. The degree of roasting is important – do you want a full-on dark roast or a softer, lighter one? The bean or blend of bean you'll need will require a little research. If in doubt, start experimenting with a good Costa Rican coffee. Secondly, it will need to be ground for the appropriate method of brewing, e.g. fine for filter, medium for cafetiere.

Thirdly, it's most important to use the right amount. Even if you have measured it about right, you can still muck it up by putting too much water through. This will produce weak coffee, which is pointless, and also tastes bitter because you've over-extracted it, letting the bitter part of the bean get into the brew. We recommend 2 heaped tbsp ground coffee per 250ml of water.

The water temperature is also crucial, for unlike tea, which requires boiling water for infusion, coffee will scorch if this is used. It destroys the delicate aromatic oils, leaving a burnt taste. The water should be just off the boil, at about 97°C.

BAKED POTATO WITH CAVIAR

NOSH *PANFORTE DI SIENA*

NYC-STYLE CREAMED POTATO

THE ULTIMATE CLUB SANDWICH

CHEESE-OF-ALL-CHEESES

FRENCH BEANS WITH ROAST GARLIC

CHILLI AÏOLI

HOME-MADE CRISPS

FRESH OYSTERS WITH SHALLOT VINEGAR
AND JALAPEŇO PEPPER SAUCE

Simply Indulgent

'The taking of one's pleasure freely' as far as food is a spontaneous reaction to the lusty demands of the taste buds. It doesn't necessarily depend on complicated or involved procedures. People often assume that when we are peckish at home, as cooks we conjure up handmade pastas with involved sauces. How wrong they are. More often than not, as any chef will tell you, a quick snack is more likely to be some mature cheese melted on a baguette or some cold meats with a good choice of mustards. These are the foods that sustain and appeal.

How many of us remember that fish bouillon from our holiday in Geneva? It's more often granny's pie crust or mother's gravy that our taste buds recall with mouthwatering fondness.

Heaven can be as much in a simple 'garbure' (or thick peasant soup) of winter vegetables as in any complex, rich dish, and more than in any other part of this book we intend to show here that 'indulgence' doesn't have to mean 'complicated'.

A simple baked potato, Noshed up, highlights this perfectly.

Baked potato
with caviar

SERVES 2

Fish with potatoes, in a number of per-
mutations, is the mainstay of the Nordic
countries. As is often the case, the simplest
peasant dishes are the most memorable.
The caviar served with this the first time
we ate it in Gothenburg was small moist
orangey-red fish eggs called 'Löj rom',
which I suspect was probably native to
the Nordic coastline. It's difficult to find
outside those shores, so we have substi-
tuted Beluga caviar, regarded as the
mother of all caviars – and certainly our
favourite. (Oscietra or Sevruga will also do
nicely.) Look for 'malossol' on the label,
which indicates low saltiness, and is a
guide to top quality. There is quite a lot of
Iranian caviar for sale now, as well as the
traditional Russian varieties, and generally
it is quite good.

As for the potatoes, by all means start
off the baking process in a microwave
(indeed this is one of the few times it's
useful – as it heats from the inside out, the
middle of the potato won't have to be
hard) – but it's imperative to complete the
process in a regular oven to get the skin
nice and crispy. A floury variety, such as
Maris Piper or King Edward, is to be
preferred.

2 × 250g baking potatoes, scrubbed clean
Maldon sea salt and freshly ground black
    pepper
60g unsalted butter, cubed
150ml soured cream
150g best Beluga caviar

Method

Dry and prick the potatoes and bake in a hot oven (230°C/450°F/gas mark 8) for about 45–55 minutes, starting the potatoes off in a microwave (on 'high' setting) for the first 4–8 minutes or so if you want.

When they're soft in the very middle, split the potatoes along their length and season with salt and pepper. Dot with a couple of cubes of the butter and swirl a couple of large tablespoons of soured cream into the split. You should note that the best type is the runny cream, prepared in the Eastern European tradition, not the stiff crème fraiche found in France.

Quickly divide the caviar between each potato — and the dish is ready. Some people favour chopped egg or onion as additional garnishes, but in this instance it detracts from the simple appeal of the idea.

Nosh panforte di Siena

CUTS INTO ABOUT 20–25 PIECES

This Italian dried fruit-and-nut cake, a speciality of the region of Siena in Tuscany, is a great favourite of ours to accompany coffee. It has more depth of flavour than any biscuit; it is less sweet and lasts longer. (Wrapped in foil and kept airtight, it will stay in good condition for weeks and does not need to be refrigerated.)

We have adapted the basic recipe, which consists of mixed dried fruit and nuts, discarding dried pineapple but including figs and a hint of cloves to produce a heavy musky flavour. Rice-paper is the traditional covering for exported panforte (home-made versions only needing icing sugar to serve); we think rice-paper makes for ease of handling wherever you are, and helps with the sense of occasion. We are indebted to Anna Longaretti for the inspiration for this Italian delight.

120g blanched skinned almonds
120g hazelnuts
60g glacé apricots, chopped
60g dried figs, chopped
60g candied mixed peel
30g plain flour, sifted
2 tbsp cocoa powder, sifted
1 tsp powdered cinnamon
1 level tsp powdered cloves
hazelnut oil
60g dark chocolate

2 tbsp soft dark brown sugar
4 tbsp strong-flavoured honey (Greek
  mountain or Mexican)

TO SERVE
icing sugar
rice-paper (to shape)

Method

Spread the nuts on a baking tray and roast for 5 minutes or so in a warm oven (160°C/325°F/gas mark 3), until they're lightly golden brown. Chop them roughly and add to the apricots, figs, peel, flour, cocoa powder, cinnamon and cloves and mix well.

Lightly oil a 23cm springform tin with hazelnut oil and line the bottom and sides with greaseproof-paper strips.

Melt the chocolate in a bowl over hot water, and in a saucepan melt the sugar in the honey, then bring to the boil and sim-mer for 5 minutes or so until a few drops form a soft ball in cold water. Now add to the fruit/nut mix and stir around. Then add the melted chocolate and stir around thoroughly.

Pour the mixture into the springform tin and spread around evenly over the base, then bake in a cool oven (150C/300°F/gas mark 2) for 35 minutes. Remove from the oven and cool. After 10 minutes or so, remove the sides and the greaseproof paper and place the disc of cake onto a rice-paper base. Line the edge with a narrow strip of rice-paper, finishing the top with another large disc of paper to match the base.

Press down to seal and allow to cool completely. The disc will resemble a white paper cake-stand, but about 1–2cm high. When cold, it can be cut with a very sharp knife into thin wedges to go with after-dinner coffee.

If desired, you can just place a rice-paper disc on the bottom edge and sift icing sugar onto the top before serving.

NYC-style creamed potato

Nick has a particular fondness for this dish. At the River Café on the Brooklyn side of New York's East River, it was particularly memorable as a side dish with fish. The topping of butter and spring onions had been lightly grilled. It wasn't obvious whether this was a delib-erate act or simply the result of the service team's 'holding pattern' whereby the dish was probably kept piping hot under a grill until the fish was ready. Either way, it was simple yet masterful, and we unashamedly reproduce it here for you to enjoy (on its own, if necessary!). Neither fish nor Brooklyn are prerequi-sites.

1.8 kg old floury potatoes, peeled and cut into
    even-sized pieces
Maldon sea salt
75 ml single cream
freshly ground black pepper
60g slightly salted butter

TO SERVE
melted butter
chopped spring onions

Method

Boil the potatoes in salted water until tender, then drain and mash using a mouli* or sieve. Over very gentle heat, stir in the single cream, and season with salt and pepper. Add the butter, and stir in.

Pile into an ovenproof bowl, brush with melted butter and sprinkle liberally with spring onions. Place under a medium hot grill for a couple of minutes to brown the topping very slightly. Serve piping hot.

* Do not use a power whisk, as this disintegrates the starch cells in the potato and creates a gluey-textured paste.

The ultimate club sandwich

SERVES 1

If you're fairly hungry and don't want a typical 'sit-down' meal but nonetheless need something more than a simple sandwich, the club sandwich is always a brilliant idea. More often than not, though, there are elements that, improperly done, spoil the gastronomic experience. Like brown bread or bread with hard-to-eat grainy seeds in. Or chewy bacon, or the rind left on so that with one bite you empty the mayonnaise and tomato onto your shirtfront. Maybe the salad is badly drained lollo rosso, tasting like a wet flannel. All the different components of the sandwich leaves a lot of leeway for mistakes.

Here we have used focaccia, which toasts up very well, guinea fowl, stronger in flavour than supermarket chicken, and pancetta – the Italian dry-cure process ensures a good flavour without too much saltiness. The salad should comprise a tasty green element, some mayo and a thin slice of tomato. It goes without saying that you'll need decent salad leaves, and the tomato should be strong-flavoured, without a woody interior and definitely no skin. Otherwise, one chew and we're

Indulgence
36

back to mayonnaise on shirt territory again!

Focaccia is to the late 90s what baguettes were to the 70s. The vogue for all things Italian didn't come a moment too late for us. Focaccia is a welcome change from the dry baguettes that plagued us then as it has both moistness and flavour from the olive oil. Here we give a recipe for preparing your own. You can adapt it by adding olives, or rosemary or, say, fine sliced onion on the base – experiment with your favourite flavours.

1 slab focaccia 20 × 20cm (see page 39)
4 leaves red oak-leaf lettuce
4 small leaves rocket
2 large fully ripe firm Italian plum tomatoes, skinned
1 breast free-range guinea fowl
1 tsp good-quality olive oil
Maldon sea salt and freshly ground white pepper
3 thinly sliced rashers Italian pancetta
1 tbsp thick mayonnaise (see page 40)

Focaccia method

Make the bread as described on page 40 or buy some (it's not the same, though).

Salad method

Using fresh ingredients ensures a good result. Red oak-leaf lettuce or batavia is decent although you can get new exotic salad leaves like shungiko (a dwarf chrysanthemum) and mizuna, or the very esoteric types like texel, tatsai, gold orach, serrated santo, celtuce and jaba. A little rocket is fine but don't use too much or the taste will dominate the dish. Green salad should be picked clean, washed and drained. It is vital that it is dry and that the tomatoes are skinned and sliced thinly.

One of our favourite tastes is young pea shoots – pea seeds, sprouted and grown to a height of about 7–10cm and then cropped. They have all the juicy sweetness of the pea flavour with crunchy, juicy leaves.

– Always try to use young leaves, older ones have a coarseness you don't want.
– When washing leaves, replenish the water several times: it only takes one piece of grit to spoil the whole dish. And remember to drain and dry them thoroughly – a toss in a dry tea towel is quite effective if you're in a hurry.
– Cut the leaves don't tear them: tearing causes the edges of the leaves to oxidize and go brown. Remember not to toss in the dressing until you need to serve – otherwise it will wilt the leaves. Don't use lollo rosso. It is a limp-wristed, tasteless lettuce that will not enhance any salad (although lollo biancho, the plain version, is not too bad).

If you're using purslane, radicchio, dandelion, claytonia, or frisée (curly endive) be very sparing, as these leaves have a bitter or sour taste and will dominate the sandwich flavours.

Guinea fowl method

Trim the breast of all fatty bits and strip off the skin and discard it. (The skin does have a great taste but unfortunately, if cooked and included in the sandwich, it will, if bitten, assist the collapse of the layers and allow the meat layer to be dragged out.)

Simply oil the breast, season with salt and white pepper and pan-fry or grill it until just done; for an average-sized breast this will be about 4 minutes or so each side. The exact time will depend on how plump you leave your meat; flattening it before cooking with the palm of your hand will ensure quick cooking. Leave to rest, on a clean board, until any pink juices have set and run clear.

When tepid, cut across the breast thinly into 3mm slices ready for assembly.

Pancetta method

Ensure your rashers are thinly sliced – it's better to have a couple of thin slices than one thick one.

With kitchen scissors snip away the rind and some of the adjoining fat (don't cut it *all* away – that's where a lot of the flavour is), then along the edge of the fat at 5mm intervals to help prevent the rasher curling up. Grill or pan-fry until well done but not so crispy that you can't eat the bacon without shattering it. (If frying you can keep the pancetta flat by placing a small saucepan on top of it.)

Assembly

Toast the focaccia lightly on both sides and cut it horizontally into three equal slices. Spread a thin layer of mayo on the cut edge of the top bottom slice and both sides of the middle slice. (This is the glue that holds it all together.) Try building from the bottom up with layers thus (but don't be afraid to vary the combinations as you wish): focaccia, mayo, oak-leaf lettuce, tomato, seasoning, pancetta, rocket, mayo, focaccia, mayo, oak-leaf lettuce, tomato, seasoning, guinea fowl slices, rocket, mayo, focaccia. Eat, enjoy!

Focaccia

MAKES ONE 32 × 22 CM LOAF TO SERVE 10 APPROX.

250g strong white bread flour
150ml tepid spring water
½ sachet dried easy-blend yeast

25ml olive oil
a pinch of Italian herbs (oregano, thyme, basil)
1 level tsp Maldon sea salt

Method

Put half the flour into a large bowl with all the water, and mix. Cover with a tea towel and leave at room temperature overnight (at least 12 hours).

In another bowl mix the remainder of the flour with the yeast and the rested overnight flour/water mix, and stir until well combined. Next, mix in the olive oil and herbs, then knead the dough on a lightly floured surface. Add a little more flour or water to adjust the texture of the dough: it should feel slack. (When formed into a ball it should not stay in a ball but rather spread out slightly.) Do not add too much flour.

Mix by hand, about 15 minutes, or if you are lazy like us, in a mixer for 10 minutes. In the last 5 minutes add the salt. Form into a ball, place in a greased plastic bag and blow it up. Twist the top into a knot to seal it, and let it prove in a warm, not hot, place for 1 hour until it has doubled in size. (Alternatively, a cling-filmed bowl will do.)

Take the inflated risen dough and punch it down. Form it into a ball again, and let it rest for another 15 minutes.

Place the dough on a floured board and make into a rectangular shape, to fit a greased 2.5cm deep bakewell pan. Place it upside down in the tin and press hard with your fingertips all over the surface to make a dimpled surface about 1cm deep. Put the covered tray in a warm place (the plastic bag routine works well again), and leave for about 1 hour to double in size once more. Don't knock or bang the tin or surface, as it may deflate the dough and ruin your efforts. Halfway through your waiting time, preheat the oven to 220°C/425°F/gas mark 7.

Sprinkle the surface of the focaccia with some more salt, place the tin in the oven and reduce the temperature immediately to 170°C/ 340°F/gas mark 3–4 for 25–30 minutes. You can cover the top of the bread with foil to prevent any edges burning if required. Let cool for 3 hours before cutting.

It seems like a lot of work, but we guarantee it will be delicious and worth your while.

Mayonnaise

MAKES ABOUT 600ML

300ml good-quality olive oil
300ml good-quality salad oil (sunflower, etc.,
    but not soya)

3 small egg yolks
Maldon sea salt
1 tsp good-quality Dijon mustard

1 tsp lemon juice
1 tbsp white wine vinegar
freshly ground black pepper
a pinch of caster sugar

Method

Mix the oils. Whisk the egg yolks with some salt and the mustard, then pour in half the mixed oils, incorporating them thoroughly and beating all the time, then add the lemon juice and vinegar and continue to pour and whisk the oil in. Finally adjust the seasoning, adding salt, pepper and sugar if necessary. If the mayonnaise looks too thin or has split and curdled, it is possible to rescue it by beating another yolk in a separate bowl and pouring the original mixture in gradually, beating well as before, but really taking plenty of time to whisk well together.

Cheese-of-all-cheeses

SERVES 4–6

Nobody in their right mind would buy just one or two cheeses for a decent selection. That's the dilemma – which ones to buy when you want them all – as well as avoiding all the scrappy waste? Here's something we have invented for the discerning cheese aficionado – the cheese of-all-cheeses. It's the height of indulgence taste-wise. You simply combine any number of cheeses and leave them for a short while to mature, with a few drops of cream for moisture, and maybe some chives or some truffle oil, if desired. The beauty of it is that you can vary your accompaniments as much as the original selection. The random selection of cheeses is all part of achieving a novel result, but use your common sense as well as your taste buds to decide what goes best with each cheese. For example, it would be excessive to add garlic to your mix if your cheese selection already has Boursin in it. Experiment and enjoy!

450g of cheese in 50g slices (say, Cheddar, Brie, Cheshire, Wensleydale, Cashel Blue, Roquefort, Gruyère), cut into chunks; chill the softer varieties well, in a freezer if necessary, for ease in handling
2 tbsp single cream (optional)
a little crushed garlic or snipped chives (optional)
1 tsp truffle oil

Method

You will need a clean muslin cloth to wrap the cheese in, and a form to shape it in (a Chinese bamboo 'dim sum' steamer basket is ideal as a mould, as it will allow air in at both top and bottom).

Remove all the rinds (hard and soft) and grate all the cheese on a coarse grater (you can use a grater attachment on a food processor if desired, but take care not to over-process into a mush). You should aim for a coarse texture that allows you to recognize one cheese, then another, and another in your mouth as you taste the whole piece. Using your hands (or a bread-dough hook attachment of a processor), combine all the cheese fragments into one lump, which can be loosely bound with a spoonful or two of cream if needed, or a little crushed garlic or chives. (Don't overdo this part: if it's dry, add cream; if bland, add extra flavour.) Shape the block into a cylinder and cover with the cloth. Place it in the bamboo mould and press down on the top to make a smooth flat rind. Prick the top a few times with a skewer and pour about half a spoonful of truffle oil into the holes to enrich and moisten the cheese-of-all-cheeses. Fold the cloth over to seal the block and place it in the fridge for about 3 days, then unfold the cloth, pour the remainder of the truffle oil over and replace the cloth. After another 3–4 days the cheese flavours should have amalgamated and it will be ready. To serve, let it warm up to room temperature, cut a sliver and taste.

French beans with roast garlic

SERVES 8

This is intended as a fully-loaded side dish. If served with say, lamb, it may be sufficiently robust for you to dispense with the potatoes.

Most fine green beans seem to be imported from Kenya these days. If you can, get the fatter English beans called 'bobby beans' – they have some real body! Kenyan beans tend to look good, but have minimal taste.

1.4kg green beans
60g butter

1 whole bulb garlic
1 tbsp virgin olive oil
Maldon sea salt and freshly ground black pepper

Method

Simply roast the whole bulb of garlic in a hot oven (220°C/425°F/gas mark 7) for 15–20 minutes until the skin is dark brown in places. Cool, then squeeze out the garlic flesh, clove by clove. The cooked garlic will have a creamy-brown colour and soft consistency (and will keep in a spoonful of virgin oil if not using straightaway). Roast garlic has a sweetness all of its own and goes very well here with the beans and extremely well with NYC-style creamed potato (page 35).

Trim and string the beans, then simmer or steam until tender. Toss with the butter and roast garlic cloves in oil, then season with salt and pepper.

Chilli aïoli

SERVES 8

Like most dips and sauces, quality of taste depends on the quality of ingredients. Use the freshest produce for the optimum results. Although it does keep in a fridge for a couple of days aïoli benefits from being made fresh so we recommend making it as you need it. It's great with crudités and home-made crisps.

4 cloves fresh garlic, peeled
1 small red chilli, deseeded
3 small egg yolks
½ tsp Maldon sea salt
½ tsp Dijon mustard
250 ml virgin olive oil

Method

Use a food processor fitted with a chopper or blender blade. Place the garlic and chilli in the blender and chop coarsely, then add the egg yolks, salt and mustard. Keeping the motor running, pour in the oil in a steady stream until the mixture is thickened.

Test for seasoning and chill in the fridge for 1 hour to let the flavours develop.

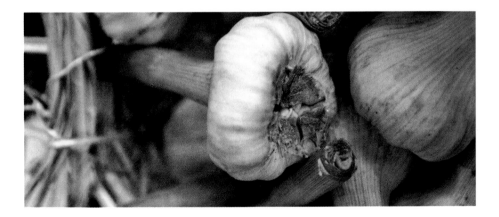

Home-made crisps

Being old enough to remember the first crisps, which came in waxpaper packets with a blue paper twist of salt, the Nosh fondness for them has never waned.

Despite most households having the simple requisites of oil, spuds and salt to hand, making crisps at home is something people rarely attempt to do – perceiving it to be too much of a fag. However, with a little preparation and including a selection of root vegetables, you can produce first-class results that would not look out of place in the Thames Foyer at the Savoy.

The trick to making good crisps is simply to avoid over-hot cooking oil – slow and steady gives a better crisp!

900g vegetables (red potatoes, parsnips, carrots, celeriac, beetroot)
new vegetable oil for deep frying (sunflower or peanut are good; no olive or soya oil, please – olive will burn and soya imparts a rank flavour)
Maldon sea salt

Method

You will need some equipment as well: a mandoline for fine-slicing the vegetables, and kitchen paper for drying the crisps.

Wash and scrub the vegetables clean,

and slice on a fine blade setting on the mandoline without peeling.

Heat the oil until fairly hot but not smoking, about 180°C/350°F (test the temperature of the oil by placing a small cube of dry white bread into it. If it sizzles, the oil is hot enough.) Place slices into the oil a small batch at a time, stirring slightly to separate the slices and stop them sticking together. Monitor the time taken and the colour – they should go a light golden brown within a few minutes. (If the oil is too hot they will darken quickly and taste bitter. If so, turn down the heat, allow to cool off for a few moments and then try another batch.)

Drain the cooked crisps in the basket for 30 seconds and then tip onto absorbent kitchen paper. Season with sea salt. Chilli aïoli (page 43) makes a good dip.

Fresh oysters with shallot vinegar and jalapeño pepper sauce

Oysters seem wrapped in mystery. Perhaps it's because of the associated allure of pearl. Actually, they've evolved from being a poor person's food into today's rather sophisticated and elevated foodstuff, but even so they're not necessarily expensive, and almost always tasty. Good varieties come from many locations but our special fondness is for those from Ireland's Galway Bay.

People who express no interest in oysters tend to object to their so-called slimy texture rather than their their taste; a few tries should convert them, and a lifetime of adoration will follow. The opening process is also easily mastered. As with any shellfish, freshness is paramount, and it's probably best to avoid those with a 'milky' aspect to their juices. They should taste firm on the bite (although many say it's sacrilegious to chew hem, and just let them 'slip down'!) and have a slightly metallic buzz on the tastebuds, which is enhanced by sharp citrus juices and the sourness of vinegar. Prepare them with this simple shallot-marinated vinegar, or use the new green Jalapeño Tabasco to inject a bit more head into the proceedings.

Decorum suggests six per person for a starter, and somewhere in the region of a dozen for a main. We have never really understood this formula. We Noshes, who devour oysters with the fervour of that reserved by others for a tube of Pringles, defy you to have 'just' half a dozen!

*Minimum 6 oysters per person (2 dozen each
would be more respectable); Belon No. 2
are recommended*

EITHER
*30g shallots or spring onion, finely chopped
6 tbsp fine champagne vinegar
a dash of sherry vinegar or chilli sherry*

OR
Jalapeño hot pepper sauce (Green Tabasco)

Method

Scrub the oyster shells clean of grit and debris to ensure that during and after opening none enters the open shell or contaminates the 'pond' of juices. Hold the shell in the palm of your hand, deepest side down, to retain all the juices on opening. Sever the muscular foot-like attachment anchoring the two shells by using either the strong steel point of an oyster knife or any sharp pointed steel tip, such as an old-fashioned V-shaped juice can opener, to prise the shell open a little in order to be able to slide a knife blade along the shell's edge and cut through the muscle cleanly. The hold on the shell broken, the oyster 'relaxes'.

The traditional way to prepare the oyster is to flip the meat into the deeper half of the shell and present it in its own savoury juices, discarding the flatter top half. It is imperative that once opened the full shells are transferred to a bed of crushed ice on a serving plate, and served swiftly.

Condiments can be sprinkled on according to taste. For a traditional vinegar, place the finely chopped shallots or onion in a small ramekin dish of vinegar for 30 minutes, stirring occasionally to allow the flavours to aggregate. One of our favourite alternatives is even simpler: Tabasco's new green Jalapeño pepper sauce. Everyone knows the fiery red Tabasco, but the Jalapeño version is slightly sourer and less hot, so the perfect additional indulgence. Don't use more than a couple of drops, though: oyster flesh is very subtly flavoured, so any hot condiment should be used sparingly.

MARINATED CHARGRILLED BABY
OCTOPUS ON ROCKET SALAD

FRESH FIGS BAKED IN PARMA HAM WITH
A FRESH RASPBERRY VINAIGRETTE

CHARGRILLED CARPACCIO OF BEEF
FILLET WITH INFUSED LEMON OIL,
BLACK PEPPER AND SHAVED PARMESAN

SMOKED MUSSEL PÂTÉ WITH BRIOCHE
MELBA TOASTS

CHAMPAGNE AND CAMEMBERT SOUP
WITH ONION CROUTONS

FETTUCINE ALFREDO

TOMATO AND ROSEMARY CIABATTA

MOON-DRIED TOMATOES

ROASTED ELEPHANT GARLIC WITH
TOMATO AND ROSEMARY CIABATTA

WHITE ASPARAGUS WITH A WARM
HOLLANDAISE, SHALLOTS AND PANCETTA

KING NEPTUNE'S GAZPACHO

BASIL GNOCCHI WITH GORGONZOLA,
WHITE WINE AND PARMESAN

Start as You Mean to Go On

Time was, during our early childhood, when eating out in Britain one could only look forward to such starters as 'juices, various', 'soup du jour' or 'pâté maison'. (Did they really think that spelling the dish in French would improve it?) Asparagus was generally tinned and if picked up by hand the tip would usually fall off thanks to overboiling. Not much to look forward to – and this was meant to be the appetizer.

By the 60s a slightly more affluent feel had evolved for 'special' food, and out in the suburbs the dinner party was in full swing. The hostess trolley was born, and quiche Lorraine and egg mayonnaise appeared for starters. Meanwhile, there was much to be learned abroad. Spit-roasted rare chicken on holidays in Belgium looms large in the gastronomic memory!

The 70s saw a new direction, when more exotic produce became available. The world, it seemed, went avocado mad. We still had the basic prawn cocktail with Marie Rose sauce, but now we scooped out half an avocado to put it in.

Britain was now learning to push the boat out. Yoghurt, once the prerogative of health freaks and food faddists, was packaged with fruit, and the nation devoured it with gusto. Pasta became our friend and with post-hippy consciousness grow-your-own garden produce actually became fashionable. Once seen as a boring hobby for grandads, tending an allotment became the height of suburban chic. Seed catalogue sales boomed and gardens in Chertsey and High Wycombe sprouted *Physalis* and exotica like courgette flowers and spaghetti squash.

By the beginning of the 80s, one couldn't order a starter in a restaurant that didn't have kiwi fruit in it. We all OD'd on that one – especially since it often garnished the dessert as well. With the mid-80s boom came extra cash in our pockets, and as an antidote to that . . . Nouvelle Cuisine. Originally (and cleverly) conceived as a revolution against the old heavy sauces of Escoffier's classic traditions, the new wave promoted reductions of sauces as the current style (the best legacy of that era) and daintily executed dishes with finicky garnishes. We got 'art on a plate' . . . yet we were still hungry!

The end of that decade ushered in a recession, first perceived in despair as the end of fine dining, but actually resulting in a renaissance in British cooking. The accent on style over content faded and the combination of new young chefs and a hankering after quality fresh ingredients, simply presented, won the day. We entered the era of shaved Parmesan and sun-dried tomatoes. Complicated starters gave way to simple Mediterranean-style dishes of roasted peppers with crostinis and subtly flavoured olive oils. The cross-pollination of kitchen talent from Down Under with up-and-coming home-grown talent has resulted in a generation of food inspired by many influences. So as the sun set on the Empire, the cooking styles and influences that had shaped it came home to roost.

Thankfully we now don't have to suffer the strictures of the Victorian regime, not least when it comes to the formal starter. We have taken a leaf out of the Italians' book – a fondness for simplicity. Traditionally, the first course is intended as an appetizer, a small dish that creates aromas and flavours to coax the taste buds into life, to get the juices flowing. So nowadays we expect more than just egg mayonnaise or mushrooms à la grecque. The quality and range of salad ingredients now available means that the old British idea of salad (a slice of curled-up cucumber, a zigzag-cut tomato with a sprinkling of cress and a dollop of salad cream) is long dead, and you can probably expect a starter to include a tasty selection of salad leaves with some asparagus, artichokes, green beans, olives, lardons or even a poached egg – but with crispness, variety and usually a decent dressing (although this area still leaves room for improvement). Here in this next chapter we present a selection of modern dishes that are easy to prepare, with a full quotient of flavour on the Noshometer. Try them and enjoy!

Marinated chargrilled baby octopus on rocket salad

SERVES 4

We first tasted this dish in a wharfside restaurant in Sydney. It was divine. What's more, somebody else paid the bill! Octopus is a much underrated seafood that suffers from two drawbacks. To the conservative British eater with little experience of eating octopus it seems a scary prospect – too many suckers and childhood memories of underwater horrors from Hollywood B-movies. The second is that when fully grown it has a tendency to get rubbery and chewy – evoking Greek fishermen thrashing the poor things on a rock about eighty times to soften the flesh. The easiest way to soft flesh is the simplest – get baby octopus! They should be no bigger than your fist, and the smaller the better. While commonplace in the Med, your fishmonger will need a bit of pestering to get them in for you.

Chargrilled, they take on a good flavour and the marinade helps to infuse extra flavours into them. This can be bottled and kept for some weeks in a cool place or the fridge but we prefer to have a party and serve the lot in one go – everyone feels less squeamish about eating them when there's safety in numbers. If anyone's still unhappy about the tentacles, tell them to try the dish with their eyes closed – we guarantee they'll be hooked!

8 baby octopus – about 900g fresh weight in total
4 onions, peeled and roughly chopped
4 lemon wedges
4 bay leaves
4 sprigs parsley
6 sprigs coriander
675g ripe tomatoes, peeled, deseeded and chopped
375ml good quality olive oil
4 cloves fresh garlic, peeled and crushed
50ml lime juice
50ml red wine vinegar
2 tbsp chopped oregano
Maldon sea salt and freshly ground black pepper

TO SERVE
200g rocket leaves, washed and drained

Method

Ask your fishmonger if you are squeamish, or clean the octopus yourself: discard the head and beak, then cut the main sac open and wash out the contents under cold running water. Cut the body into strips and flatten out with a meat mallet to tenderize the flesh.

Place the octopus in boiling water with

half the onions, and the lemons, bay leaves parsley and coriander and bring to the boil. Simmer for 45–60 minutes. Remove from the heat and allow the octopus to cool in the liquid, then remove the flesh from the pan and reserve.

Now place in a large bowl the remaining onion, tomatoes, olive oil, garlic, lime juice, vinegar and oregano.

Chargrill the octopus pieces quickly on a hot grill, and place warm into the oil marinade. Mix well and store in the fridge overnight. Remove from the fridge at least one hour before serving.

Season to taste, and serve on rocket salad.

Fresh figs baked in Parma ham with a fresh raspberry vinaigrette

SERVES 6

This dish is typical of the new wave of 90s cooking. It combines Italian simplicity with the vogue for lighter sauces (here, combining fresh fruits with traditional salad dressings). Using prime-quality Parma ham and fresh figs, it lets the ingredients speak for themselves, creating a starter that both looks good and tastes good, while leaving room for more pleasures later! What more could one desire?

175 g fresh raspberries
2 tbsp balsamic vinegar
120 ml olive oil
Maldon sea salt and freshly ground black pepper
12 large fresh figs
6 slices Parma ham, cut in half lengthways
50 ml cognac

Method

Preheat oven to 150°C/300°F/gas mark 2.

Place the raspberries and vinegar in a blender and blitz until smooth. Keeping the motor running, pour in the oil in a thin steady stream until combined, then season and reserve.

Next, cut a small cross in the top of each fig, and wrap a collar of Parma ham around it. Place in a shallow baking tray, sprinkle with the cognac and put it in the oven for 8–10 minutes or so (take care not to overdo the fruits otherwise the ham will crisp up and frizzle). Serve warm with the raspberry dressing sprinkled over the fruits.

Chargrilled carpaccio of beef fillet with infused lemon oil, black pepper and shaved Parmesan

SERVES ABOUT 16

Most people like the taste of a well char-grilled beef 'crust' counterpointed with a pink centre. We have adapted the traditional Italian starter of raw beef fillet slices by partially grilling the fillet before slicing. It's the best of both worlds!

1 beef fillet (cut into a neat cylinder, about
    20cm long – ask your butcher to larder
    trim it, removing the chain and sinew)
3 tbsp olive oil
Maldon sea salt and freshly ground black pepper
infused lemon oil, made with extra-virgin
    olive oil (see below)
120g wedge best Parmesan

Carpaccio method

Chill the fillet in the fridge for at least 2 hours. Take it out and brush with plain olive oil, season and place on a very hot barbecue grill. Turn the fillet, rolling it to chargrill it evenly all over for about 2–3 minutes for each section. Once done, place the meat on a dish to cool and rest, allowing some juices to seep out. When somewhat cooler (about 30 minutes later), wrap it in a large sheet of clingfilm, then foil, twisting each end tightly like a sweet wrapper to squeeze it into a neat, compact shape. Then place in the fridge for at least 2 hours to chill and firm up.

When ready to serve, unwrap the beef and slice into thin discs (an electric slicer is invaluable here) – but no more than 30 minutes before serving, as this prevents the meat drying out and curling up. Sprinkle lemon oil drops around each serving, a pinch of salt and black pepper and finally thin shavings from the length of the wedge of Parmesan.

Infused lemon oil method

You can buy ready-made lemon-infused olive oil ready for pouring, but it's easily made at home. Simply blanch whole fresh unwaxed or organic lemons in boiling water for a few minutes (this enables any residual waxy coating to be cleaned off with a dry cloth and ensures a sterile outer skin) then cut into wedges and push them into a sterile clear glass bottle (an old empty olive oil bottle is fine). The best oil to use is a medium-weight olive oil that has a smooth, even light, not peppery, flavour, like Sicilian Ravida. (Some of the greeny virgin first pressings are too strong in flavour and will mask the delicacy.) Cap the bottle with a stainless steel and cork drinks pourer and you will have a lemon oil for dressing fish or other foods within a week. So long as you can keep the lemon slices immersed in the oil, they will not get furry with mildews. The taste can be further accentuated by steeping peeled inner stems of lemon grass in the oil – which gives an oriental taste.

Smoked mussel pâté with brioche Melba toasts

SERVES 8

Smoked mussels have been around for a long time – if memory serves, at least since the 60s, packed in oil in tins like sardines. However, unlike fishpaste sandwiches, they have stood the test of time, and served on sticks, handed around at cocktail parties they have a very rich taste. It lends itself to a simple pâté.

For best results, use a terrine dish that actually has folding sides.

Melba toast is a distinctly 60s thing, which we have updated by using brioche loaf.

1 tbsp virgin olive oil
60g shallots, finely chopped
1 clove garlic, crushed
60ml double cream
1 medium egg
1 tsp ground cumin
8 × 60g tins of smoked mussels, drained
juice of ½ a lemon

Maldon sea salt and freshly ground black pepper
melted butter

TO SERVE
1 brioche loaf

Method

Heat the olive oil on a low flame and pan-fry the chopped shallots for 2–3 minutes until softened, adding the garlic after 1 minute or so. Do not let the mixture brown – just cook until transparent. Set aside.

Place the cream, egg, cumin and mussels in a blender and process with a few short pulses to blend together. Season lightly and add the reserved shallots and garlic. Squeeze in the lemon juice to cut through the richness, and with a spatula scoop the mixture into a 26cm terrine tin lined with clingfilm.

Wrap a foil lid tightly over the top and place in a hot-water bain-marie (it is essential that the clingfilm makes a water-tight seal around the pâté mix). Bake in the oven for 20–25 minutes at 160°C/325°F/gas mark 3). Remember, the mussels have been hot-smoked already, so they don't need a lot of cooking – simply setting with the egg/cream mixture.

Remove from the oven, take out of the bain-marie and allow to cool quickly (a fork under one end of the terrine will enable cool air to circulate under the tin).

When cool, firm up in the fridge for a couple of hours.

To make the Melba toasts, simply cut the brioche loaf into 5mm slices and remove the crusts, then lightly toast each slice on both sides flat on a grill tray. When cool, use a very sharp knife to cut each slice into halves so that you end up with two identical thin slices each 2–3mm thick and now only toasted on one side. Finally, place each new untoasted side uppermost cut into triangular halves on the grill tray and toast the cut side lightly until done. Being thinly cut, each piece will tend to curl up somewhat – this is perfectly OK and you should end up with some crisp tasty triangles which are perfect for spreading your pâté.

Champagne and Camembert soup with onion croutons

SERVES 4

Nick remembers this as one superb dining experience from a twenty-first birthday party, years ago. Unable to retrace the steps to the original recipe, we have experimented endlessly to clone his dish from memory and we faithfully reproduce our findings here. They're rather good . . .

CROUTONS
1 small strong white onion, peeled, sliced and finely diced
3 tbsp olive oil
2 slices stale white bread, cubed

Maldon sea salt and freshly ground black pepper

90g shallots, peeled and finely chopped
1 small old potato, peeled and finely diced
1 tbsp olive oil
1 small knob unsalted butter
1 clove garlic, peeled and crushed
225ml champagne
600ml chicken stock (see page 57)
120g ripe Camembert cheese (rind off), diced
90ml single cream
Maldon sea salt and freshly ground black pepper

Crouton method

Fry the onion slowly over a low heat in the olive oil until light brown and beginning to go crispy. Now add the cubes of bread and turn rapidly to absorb the oniony oil, so that the onion sticks to the croutons. When the oil is absorbed, transfer the croutons to a foil-covered baking tray and bake in the oven at 160°C/325°F/gas mark 3 for a few minutes until golden brown in colour. This way, you only need a small amount of cooking oil to complete the process, as it is rapidly absorbed by the bread. Drain on kitchen paper and keep warm.

Soup method

Soften the shallots and potato in the olive oil and butter over a low heat, adding the crushed garlic after some minutes (do not allow the garlic to turn brown or it may turn bitter).

Pour in the champagne, bubble for one minute to allow the alcohol to boil off, then add the stock and bring to the boil. Turn down to a simmer for 15–20 minutes to allow the potato to break down and thicken the soup, then add the cheese, allowing it to melt.

Simmer for 3 minutes, then add the cream, check the seasoning and simmer for another 2–3 minutes to allow the flavours to mingle.

Finally, serve in warmed deep soup plates with the croutons.

Chicken Stock

MAKES 1 LITRE

2 fresh tomatoes, deseeded and diced
1 large shallot, diced
120g carrots, diced
3 sticks celery, diced
1 large Spanish onion, diced
120g mushrooms, diced
2 whole cloves garlic, crushed
1 tsp chervil leaves
a handful of parsley stalks
½ bottle dry white wine

2 litres cold water
450g raw chicken wings
1kg raw chicken carcass and bones
2 thick rashers bacon, rind on

Method

Place all the vegetables with the herbs, wine and water in a large pot, and bring to the boil. When it comes to the boil, add the chicken wings, carcass and bones and bacon.

Let it cook slowly uncovered for 4 hours, skimming off any scum, froth or fat that floats to the top. Then strain through a very fine sieve, return the liquid to the pan and reduce volume by a quarter. Allow to cool, then put the cooled stock into a large plastic container and refrigerate. Any fat that remains will come to the surface and can be skimmed off.

If you want a rich glaze for a piece of meat, simply reduce 300ml of stock on a very low heat to about an eighth of its original volume (or less) – the liquid should then coat the back of a spoon and will be smooth with a glistening shine.

But remember, as you reduce a solution, the saltiness increases proportionately, so don't add seasonings until the end.

Fettucine Alfredo

SERVES 4

Fettucine is the Roman tagliatelle, slightly narrower (about 8mm) and slightly thicker. It makes an excellent vehicle for this rich starter, for in Italy, pasta is usually eaten as a first course, seldom as a main. The sauce with it is a classic cream sauce. It also makes a great lunch dish served with a green salad and a bottle of chilled Montagny premier cru. You could also add some crispy lardons just at the end for no other reason than unbridled extravagance.

900g fresh egg fettucine
Maldon sea salt
400ml double cream
60g unsalted butter, cubed
170g Parmesan, grated
freshly ground black pepper

Method

Cook the fettucine in plenty of boiling salted water until al dente.

Heat the cream in a saucepan and simmer for 1 minute. Drain the cooked pasta, add the butter and toss around, and add to the cream, turning it for a few minutes over a low heat. Season and add the cheese, tossing again to coat the pasta evenly.

Serve direct from the pan with a good couple of grinds of black pepper.

Roasted elephant garlic
with tomato and rosemary ciabatta

Giant or elephant garlic is in season around late spring and early summer and makes a strong tasting yet light starter. The idea is to roast the garlic bulbs whole and then serve them with the tops cut off – dip yer bread in!

4 giant elephant garlic bulbs, whole, unpeeled
1 fresh ciabatta loaf (see page 60)

Method

Make the ciabatta first (see page 60). You can bake the garlic at the same time.

Preheat the oven to 220°C/425°F/gas mark 7. Place the garlic on a metal roasting tray, and bake for about 20–25 minutes on the middle shelf until the skins have browned and the flesh of the bulbs is soft. Remove from the oven, allow to cool, and cut off the top, rather like a boiled egg, to expose the roasted segments. Then it's a simple matter of dipping in a small coffeespoon or knife to scoop out the sweet flesh. Smear it on slices of the hot ciabatta. It is heavenly!

Tomato and rosemary ciabatta

SERVES 4

Ciabatta (literally 'slipper') is an olive-oil bread from Italy, the recipe for which can easily be adapted to carry any or many of a variety of herbs or cheeses to flavour it. The unique detail of ciabatta is that the dough, once risen, is not knocked back into a smooth close texture but is left open, resulting in a crisp crust with large holes which gives the loaf a rustic feel.

450g strong plain flour
2 tsp Maldon sea salt

1 sachet easy-blend dried yeast⋆
250 ml hand-warm water
4 tbsp virgin olive oil
freshly ground black pepper
2 tbsp of the moon-dried tomatoes' preserving
  olive oil
6 moon-dried tomatoes (see page 61)
2 tbsp chopped fresh rosemary

Method

Sift the flour into a warm mixing bowl, add 2 tsp salt and yeast, and make a well in the centre. Pour in the water and 3 tbsp of the olive oil, drawing in the flour gradually. Knead the dough until smooth and elastic, about 5 minutes. Place in a floured bowl, cover with clingfilm and put the bowl in a warm place for 1 hour, or until the dough has doubled in size.

Then shape the ciabatta dough into a flat oval and paint with the tomato olive oil. Chop the tomatoes into a fine pulp and spread over the middle section of the dough. Season lightly with salt and freshly ground black pepper and sprinkle liberally with half the rosemary.

Fold one long edge of the dough over the filling, then the other edge, to make a loaf shape and place, fold side down, on a floured baking tray which has been lightly sprinkled with some of the remaining rosemary. Paint the top of the loaf dough with the remaining olive oil and sprinkle the last of the rosemary on top. Sprinkle finally with some more sea salt and bake in the oven at 200°C/400°F/gas mark 6 for 25–30 minutes depending on the thickness of the dough.

Allow to cool slightly before cutting, but this bread is best served warm. If reheating from cold, warm for 5–10 minutes in the oven at 180°C/350°F/gas mark 4) oven before serving.

⋆ Modern active dried yeasts mean that we can mix the yeast directly into the flour without having to make a starter mix, which saves time. If you feel like being a purist, there is nothing wrong with using fresh yeast, which is easily obtainable from any good health-food store's refrigerated section. But we reckon the new dried easy-blend stuff is fine.

Moon-dried tomatoes

We call these 'moon-dried tomatoes' in deference to the outdoor sun-dried Italian imports. You can make them easily in you own home . . . while you sleep . . . literally! You must have the plum type of Italian tomatoes. It doesn't matter if they are a bit overripe or bruised, in fact this recipe is perfect for tomatoes that are a bit squishy or 'over' for fresh salads.

Method

Wash the tomatoes and dry them. Next, cut horizontally along the long centre line of the tomato (bisecting it from stem point north to south). If the stem end has a very white hard pith core, remove it with a sharp paring knife and discard it. Arrange the tomato halves cut side up on a wire cake rack (*not* on a flat baking tray, as they will tend to burn on the bottom surface). Brush each cut surface with olive oil and season with sea salt and a twist of freshly ground black pepper.

Bake overnight in a very, very low oven (50°C/125°F/the very lowest gas) until they have dried out and shrivelled somewhat. In Italy the tradition is to remove the seeds and core, which gives a dryish, chewy result; with the watery core left in, there is a moister feel on the palate.

This is a dish that can be made after you have baked something in the oven on a high heat. All you have to do is to switch the oven off, place the racks of tomatoes inside and shut the door. The natural decrease in temperature will accommodate the process needed for best results. If you have an Aga solid-top-type oven, the plate-warming cupboard section is best for this. You may need to keep the tomatoes in for 24 hours! Keep an eye on them. Slow and even is the way.

When the tomatoes have finished their drying out process, they can be preserved in a Kilner jar of good quality olive oil. The oil itself can be flavoured with garlic and various herbs such as thyme to vary the results. So long as the dried tomatoes are covered they will not become mildewed. They will keep for a couple of months in a cold place and about six months in a cold fridge. The oil will then solidify so thaw it out if you just want to remove a couple of tomatoes for a single dish.

White asparagus with a warm hollandaise, shallots and pancetta

SERVES 6

White asparagus is simply green asparagus that is cut below ground before the emerging tips have a chance to go green on exposure to the sun. The blanched spear has an altogether different taste and texture and is widely regarded on the

Continent – especially in Germany – as a great delicacy. The season is very short (really only April) and you may have to seek out a good supplier, but as with all new fashions in food, some degree of demand soon makes an impact on vegetable suppliers and in time supermarkets. Try to get some – it's delicious!

24 finger-thick spears of white asparagus
6 large 'banana' shallots, peeled and finely chopped
15g unsalted butter
6 fine slices Italian smoked pancetta, cut into lardons
1 tbsp olive oil

HOLLANDAISE SAUCE
4 tbsp white wine vinegar
12 red peppercorns
2 bay leaves
a pinch of Maldon sea salt
3 egg yolks
a pinch of cayenne pepper
80–150g softened unsalted butter
lemon juice

Hollandaise method

Pour into a small saucepan the white wine vinegar, the peppercorns, the bay leaves, and sea salt, and bring to the boil. Simmer to reduce by half. Strain into a cup, reserving the peppercorns, and allow to cool to blood heat.

Place the egg yolks, the cayenne pepper and the strained liquid in a bowl over a hot water bain-marie, and add the butter in walnut-sized lumps, whisking continuously until the sauce thickens. (Do not allow the sauce to boil or contact the hot water underneath or it will curdle.) Stir in the reserved peppercorns, season with lemon juice and keep warm until required for serving (no longer than 10 minutes or it will split).

Asparagus method

Bring 5cm of lightly salted water to the boil in an asparagus kettle and simmer–steam the asparagus for about 3 minutes (the tops will be cooked purely in the steam). Try one at the bottom after about 2 minutes to ensure they're not cooked to a mush. Drain and reserve.

Meanwhile, sauté the shallots in the butter until soft and the pancetta in the olive oil until crisp. Mix the shallots into the warm hollandaise, pour the sauce over the base of each asparagus spear, then garnish with the crisp pancetta lardons and serve.

King Neptune's gazpacho

SERVES 4

Gazpacho is one of our favourite dishes for a hot summer's day. Liking both seafood salads and marinated seafood, we thought we could combine the two ideas – after all, what is gazpacho but marinated vegetables? We replaced the balsamic vinegar of the traditional gazpacho with lime juice to give that sharp flavour, and folded in crab meat to give the dish some extra body. It's a dish fit for a king!

1 yellow pepper
1 long green chilli
450g large red ripe tomatoes, deseeded and chopped
½ long ridge-type cucumber, peeled, seeded and chopped
½ medium Spanish onion, peeled and chopped
1 garlic clove, peeled and chopped
450g large cooked prawns, shelled
¼ tsp fresh root ginger, finely grated
1 tbsp fresh lime juice

juice of ½ a lemon
1 tbsp extra-virgin olive oil
150 ml thick premium tomato juice
150 ml V8 vegetable juice
about 1 tbsp fresh white breadcrumbs
a large pinch of Maldon sea salt
freshly ground black pepper
½ tsp Jamaican hot pepper sauce (to taste)

TO SERVE
fresh coriander leaves
1 dressed cooked crab (at least 120g white meat)
8 jumbo prawns

Method

Roast the pepper and chilli in a preheated oven at 250°C/475°F/gas mark 9 for 5 minutes or so to blister and remove the skins (or blister them over an open flame). Cool, covered in clingfilm, in a cold bowl to loosen the skins. Skin them, deseed and core, and chop the flesh into fine dice.

Rest all the vegetables, cooked prawns and ginger in a bowl with the lime, lemon juice and olive oil for a couple of hours in the fridge. When ready to serve, blend everything together in a processor, using the tomato and V8 juices to ensure all the chunks are evenly broken down. Add the breadcrumbs and salt and pepper and whizz around for another few seconds and then taste. Add the hot sauce, gradually, so as not to overdo the heat. Don't process the soup so fine as to make it into a purée. Leave the texture slightly medium-coarse or, alternatively, process half or two-thirds of the mix very smooth and add the coarser part last to give some texture.

Keep the soup chilled until needed. Serve in chilled bowls with a few coriander leaves scattered on the top and some shredded crab meat with a couple of jumbo prawns for garnish. Some people add a cube or two of ice, but don't bother. It dilutes the soup and is only really there for effect. If the soup is well made and well chilled, it won't be in the bowl long enough to get warm!

Basil gnocchi with Gorgonzola, white wine and Parmesan

SERVES 2

Gnocchi, little potato 'cushions', are one of the most satisfying and extravagant-seeming ways of serving pasta (although not really pasta themselves). There are as many different ways of preparing them as there are regions in Italy.

Sometimes mixed with pumpkin, sometimes spinach, and often made with polenta or rice instead of potato, they are actually quite simple to create, and like most processes in the kitchen, get easier each time you do it.

Making gnocchi dough is not an exact science but you need to get the right balance between potato and flour. Too much flour and the gnocchi will be chewy and hard, too much potato and the gnocchi will fall apart and absorb too much water when boiling. So aim for a dough that is not as tough as pastry dough, more like a risen bread dough with an elastic feel to it.

The second step in making a good gnoccho is the shaping. Creating the dimples and grooves on the outside surface is part and parcel of creating a shape the sauce can cling to (see Method). Store the gnocchi on a flat floured surface sprinkled with a little polenta to prevent the pieces sticking together.

450g floury potatoes, scrubbed
120g plain flour
3 small eggs, beaten
30g soft unsalted butter
30g young basil leaves (no woody stems),
    chopped
½ tsp freshly grated nutmeg
30g Parmesan, grated
Maldon sea salt and freshly ground white
    pepper

SAUCE
300ml medium white wine
120g Gorgonzola, chopped in pieces

TO SERVE
grated Parmesan
freshly ground black pepper
finely chopped fresh parsley

Method

Boil the potatoes in their skins until just soft in the centre (prick with a sharp knife). When they are cool enough to handle, skin them and pass the flesh through a coarse-mesh mouli or sieve.

Pile the flour on a smooth table top or work surface and sieve the potato onto the top. Then make a well, and add the eggs, butter, basil, nutmeg, cheese, and salt and pepper. Mix together with a palette knife. When the mixture is well combined, use your hands (floured to prevent sticking) to mould and work the dough until consistent.

Eventually, you will have a smooth dough which can be rolled out by hand into thin sausages about 1cm in diameter. Cut on the bias every 1cm along the length of the dough sausages, and you will end up with small diamond-shaped wedges. To shape them further, push each one against the zest side of a grater (again, floured to prevent sticking) and indent with the back of a knife along the midline, pushing in far enough to make the dough look like a small cowrie shell. Take care not to make the gnocchi too large; potato pasta is quite heavy in itself and lazily cut chunky pieces will not cook properly towards the centre and will look crude and uninviting. You can, if you find it easier, roll the dough pellets along the tines of a floured dinner fork to give them some form.

Cooking is simple. Boil as you would pasta, in a large pot with plenty of well-salted water on a rolling boil. When the gnocchi float to the top, they are done! Scoop out with a perforated spoon and drain them well.

The sauce is also simple, but divinely rich. Heat the wine in a large frying pan and add the cheese, stirring around to allow it to melt into the wine. When melted, the sauce should be thick enough to coat the gnocchi and with a final sprinkling of fresh grated Parmesan, freshly ground black pepper and chopped parsley, it should be ready.

Any gnocchi that are left over after preparation will keep for a day in a fridge – but like all potato preparations, will eventually turn dry and grey. Eat them fresh is the best advice. They also go well with a rich Bolognese ragù (sauce).

THE ULTIMATE CAESAR SALAD

HOT 'SHELLFISH FRENZY'

MONSTER LOBSTER COCKTAIL

SPAGHETTI *MARINARA*
WITH GRATED *BOTTARGA*

WILD MUSHROOM RISOTTO
WITH WHITE ALBA TRUFFLE

Elegant Sufficiencies

Writing at the cusp of a new millennium, it's notable how far we've come since the formality of the last century's banquets.

In these supposedly enlightened times people don't feel so constricted by social custom and it is no longer frowned upon to, say, drink a chilled red burgundy with a fish dish. Similarly, one can serve a single dish that is a complete meal.

In this section we feature dishes substantial enough to be a main course if served in a large enough portion. On a modern restaurant menu these often sit between the starters and main courses. This is where you'll find the Caesar salad – a substantial salad with the grilled fish fillets when served in a big bowl – and perhaps a risotto, very sustaining in a large portion, and satisfying to hunger and taste buds alike.

The ultimate Caesar salad

Caesar salad, reputedly the invention of one Signor Cardini before the war, is a great and popular dish. We have kept the tang of anchovies but instead of using marinated fillets to dress the final result (which are beloved of the purist but have a slightly sour flavour from the vinegary solution they are steeped in) we have grilled and filleted fresh ones (difficult to find, but occasionally available).

Freshness is the key to a successful Caesar salad and it helps to keep the lettuce in iced water until actually needed. (Take care though, to ensure the salad leaves are dried well, so that the dressing clings properly to them.) Use very good virgin oil and make sure your egg is as fresh as you can get it. Grate your own cheese – don't use the ready-grated stuff, it's dreadful. Drink a light very cold white wine with this – an Orvieto Classico (Italy) or a Sancerre (Loire).

5 large cloves garlic, peeled
150ml virgin olive oil
6 tinned anchovy fillets, drained of oil
juice of ½ a lemon
1 tsp Dijon mustard
freshly ground black pepper
1 free-range egg yolk
2 slices white bread cut into croutons

1 cos lettuce, cleaned and drained
60g Parmesan, freshly grated
4 fresh anchovies, grilled, cooled and filleted

Method

Smash the garlic and mix it with the olive oil. Leave for 15–20 minutes, to flavour the oil.

Strain half of the oil to make the dressing. Add to it the tinned anchovies, lemon juice, mustard, pepper, and egg yolk. Whizz for half a minute or till mixed: it will be a bit like mayonnaise. Use the rest of the oil to fry the croutons in (you can add the smashed-up garlic to the frying pan but don't let it burn as that will give a bitter flavour). Drain the croutons well on a paper towel.

Toss the well-dried cos leaves with the dressing, and divide between the plates. Sprinkle with the garlic croutons and the Parmesan, then place a fresh anchovy fillet on each portion. Serve immediately, as it will not keep.

Hot 'shellfish frenzy'

SERVES 2

We find eating in France decidedly hit and miss these days. The top-level gastronomic menus are still there and worth the money, but with the modern penchant for fast food, and the French arrogance about anything not French, the middle ground has been gradually eroded and is now probably lost for ever. You used to be able to find a £10 per head meal that was memorable, but now you have to really hunt for the best places, especially in Paris.

Fortunately, one thing that is still easily available is a platter of fresh seafood, the old favourite 'plateau de fruits de mer'. We adapt the traditional dish by grilling the shellfish on a barbecue or in a griddle pan and serving them together, hot, with no accompaniment except a dish of melted butter for the lobster and some lemon wedges. Crusty bread is the only thing needed to mop up the juices.

2 large freshly cooked Scottish lobsters (tail and claw meat)
1 medium hen crab, dressed, with claws
6 king scallops, cleaned, in their shells
8 large mussels
4 large razorshell clams
6 large clams
4 large oysters
parsley
Maldon sea salt and freshly ground black pepper

TO SERVE
melted butter
crusty white bread

Method

The lobster and crab can be served warm from their well-salted boiling pot (about 8 minutes is sufficient for both) but can be reheated on a chargrill if necessary, once cooled. After boiling, the lobster tails should be split down the length with a sharp knife and the claws cracked, so the flesh can be removed easily.

The crab is cleaned by removing the small legs and discarding them, cracking the underside of the main shell and discarding the 'dead man's fingers', the grey frilly gills. The red moist flesh is as tasty as the white flesh and should be spooned up with the bread. The claws can be cracked like the lobster.

The scallops can be cooked on the half-shell, but ensure that any grit or black threads are removed first. (A little garlic salted butter with chopped parsley may help season them and stop them drying out.)

Mussels will open spontaneously when hot as will the razorshells and clams. These will not need much cooking, as the flesh is quite delicate, so take care not to dry them out. Leave the oysters uncooked.

For serving, arrange all the shellfish in their shells on a large white platter (on a special wire high tray, if you want to be authentic) and arrange the bread and butter alongside. Don't forget to supply claw crackers, shell prongs and plenty of napkins, as one of the great joys is getting your fingers well into the dish and licking them clean.

Enjoy your shellfish frenzy!

Monster lobster cocktail

SERVES 4

Lobster is one of our favourite shellfish, and has itself long been associated with extravagance and luxury. The flesh is quite full-flavoured and lends itself to rich sauces with butter and cream. Cold, it has enough substance to sustain the centre of a salad, and we have adapted this notion to a 90s update of the prawn cocktail of the 50s and 60s, now viewed with such retrospective fondness.

Lobster is relatively easy to get nowadays, imported Canadian varieties being in plentiful supply, and modern freighting methods preclude the need for freezing.

The best-tasting shellfish still come from the west coast of Scotland, however, and if you can get hold of it, it's well worth the extra expense.

4 large freshly cooked Scottish lobsters (tail and claw meat)
1 large fresh chilled crisp cos lettuce
fresh lime wedges

COCKTAIL SAUCE

150 ml freshly made thick mayonnaise (see
   page 40)
6 tbsp tomato and basil sauce
   (see page 75)
6 tbsp double cream
1 tbsp anchovy sauce (Lea and Perrins)
juice of ½ a lemon
8 large leaves basil, finely chopped
a pinch of paprika
a large dash of Tabasco sauce or chilli sherry
   (see page 75)
Maldon sea salt and freshly ground black pepper

Method

For the sauce, simply mix all the ingredients together.

We recommend a lavish presentation, for example in wide oriental soup bowls. Arrange larger salad leaves around each bowl and fill with some shredded leaves to form a base. Spoon on some of the creamy sauce and place the lobster tails around the edge of each bowl. Hang wedges of fresh limes on the bowl for squeezing.

Indulgence

Chilli sherry

This culinary secret is a good way of livening up some fish soups. It's also become a Nosh tradition for sharpening up Bloody Maries. You can also pour a few drops into risottos, gravies, soups and many sauces.

Blanch 4 large whole fresh red chillies for 15 seconds in boiling water then place them in a sterilized clear glass wine bottle. Pour over them a bottle of dry sherry, such as a fino. (Cream or medium sherries do not seem to work well with this idea.) Leave to steep for about 3 weeks.

Tomato and basil sauce

This sauce also goes well with the Spaghetti with cuttlefish and peas (page 90). And it contributes to a great seafood cocktail sauce. It freezes well and keeps in the fridge for a week.

6 × 400g tins Italian plum tomatoes
175 ml good olive oil
1 large Spanish onion, peeled and finely chopped
6 large cloves garlic, peeled and crushed
1 large bunch of fresh sweet basil, including stalks
3 tbsp dried oregano
1 tbsp caster sugar
½ tsp freshly ground white pepper
2 tsp Maldon sea salt
freshly ground black pepper
30g unsalted butter

Method

Pass the tomatoes through a mouli sieve (fine grade) to remove the seeds and skin.

Heat the olive oil in a solid-based saucepan over a medium heat and add the onion, garlic, basil and oregano.

Stir briskly to prevent the onion browning; when it has softened, add the tomato pulp. Bring the mixture to the boil and immediately reduce the heat to a low simmer. Stir in the sugar (this balances the acidity of the tomatoes), the white pepper and half the salt. Remember, as the tomato sauce reduces in volume, the degree of saltiness does too, so don't adjust the final seasoning until the end.

Simmer for about 30 minutes until well reduced. The solids will tend to condense on the bottom of the pan, so stir with a wooden spoon occasionally. The time taken for this process will vary depending on the degree of wateriness of the original tinned tomato contents, so keep an eye on it.

When the sauce is finished it should be tested for seasoning. Add the remaining salt if necessary, and remove and discard the basil (use tongs). Before using, add freshly ground black pepper, and the butter to give it a good shine. It should have a rich, thick texture.

Spaghetti marinara with grated bottarga

SERVES 8

Marinara simply means a seafood sauce, and consists mainly of some white fish, squid and shellfish cooked with some white wine and tomato and basil sauce. Whatever is in the marketplace goes into the pot.

Italian tradition forbids grated Parmesan as a topping for fish dishes, so we have come up with a novel alternative that will not upset the purist tradition, but indulges our passion for 'that bit extra': *bottarga*. A Sicilian delicacy, the locals prepare it by stuffing the fresh roe of the tuna or grey mullet into a large fresh squid and then sun-drying it. The squid and its contents shrivel until it resembles a dried stick of salami.

When fully dried it is a potent flavour enhancer (and quite expensive to buy), but fortunately a little goes a long way. First-class Italian delis should stock this gourmet treat and if you have any trouble getting a supplier, Antonio Carluccio's excellent delicatessen on Neal Street, Covent Garden, London WC2, will be able to assist.

2 small squids, cleaned,* the bodies and tentacles cut into pieces
170g firm white fish (e.g. halibut), medium diced
120g fresh salmon fillet, medium diced
12 large Scottish mussels, scrubbed
12 fresh clams, scrubbed
4 large raw prawns, head off, peeled, cleaned and halved lengthways
4 spring onions, cleaned, green 'flags' intact, diagonally cut into small dice
2 cloves garlic, peeled
4 tbsp good-quality olive oil
Maldon sea salt and freshly ground white pepper
120ml white wine
600ml freshly made tomato and basil sauce (see page 75)
30g unsalted butter
2 tbsp chopped parsley

TO SERVE
30g grated bottarga
freshly ground black pepper

Method

Set some well-salted boiling water on the hob in a large pot for the pasta. The spaghetti should take about 10 minutes to cook through, so start the *marinara* sauce immediately the pasta goes into the water.

Heat a large frying pan to medium-hot and fry the spring onions with the garlic in the olive oil for 1 minute. Then turn up the flame to high heat, add the mussels and clams and cook until they open up and release their juices into the pan; after 2 minutes they will be cooked enough to allow the lid of each shell to be twisted off and discarded. Next add the salmon, white fish, squid, and salt and pepper and cook for 1 minute. Add the prawns and when they colour up slightly pink, add the wine and turn down the heat to low. Simmer for a few minutes longer then pick out and discard the garlic cloves. Add the tomato sauce and the butter. Stir around lightly with a wooden spoon, taking care not to break up the white fish, and add the parsley.

To serve, drain the spaghetti well, and toss in the *marinara* sauce (the sauce should end up with a clinging consistency). Pile onto a large deep warmed plates and finish with a grating of *bottarga* and a generous grind of black pepper.

* To clean squid, first take off the outer purply/pink skin and discard it. Now gut the squid, cut off the head above the eyes but retain the tentacles. Remove the clear 'plastic' inner bone (actually cartilage) and wash the body free of grit. Cuttlefish are cleaned in the same way – but keep the inner 'bone' for the budgie.

Wild mushroom risotto with white Alba truffle

SERVES 8

Risotto has become so fashionable that sometimes the ingredients have become esoteric. This defeats the idea of this rustic peasant dish, making it needlessly complicated. The best additions to the rice and onion base are simple, strong tastes such as wild mushrooms, asparagus, or perhaps smoked haddock. The wrong consistency can also spoil the dish. Enough stock should be added so that it resembles a soupy pile – not sloppy or stiff. A mound served onto the plate should stand up on its own, but if the plate is shaken slightly, it should flatten out. Top-grade rice should only be used – arborio (the best variety for quality) is the label to look for. Our method isn't strictly Marcella Hazan's, but we think it still produces a dish of great integrity.

Here we have added some white Alba truffle, one of our favourite delicacies, to enhance the fungal aroma. You can use truffle oil as a substitute, but it doesn't have the luxurious effect of the original tuber. A whole truffle is expensive – maybe up to £100 – but it can be kept in dry rice (to control humidity) in a sealed plastic container for a few weeks. Pungent and strongly flavoured, it should be sliced sparingly with a potato peeler – don't overdo it, a little goes a long way!

225g fresh wild mushrooms (ceps, chanterelles, a few trompettes, Paris, blewits, etc.)
300g Arborio risotto rice
1 large onion, peeled and chopped
3 tbsp best-quality olive oil
2 tbsp salted butter
3 cloves of garlic, peeled, finely chopped and pulped
120ml white wine
450ml light chicken stock, hot (see page 57)*
Maldon sea salt and freshly ground black pepper
60ml single cream
60g Parmesan, freshly grated

TO SERVE
shavings of Parmesan
about 1 tbsp chopped parsley
1 white Alba truffle, peeled thinly, shaved thin

Method

Clean and wipe the mushrooms, rinsing if they look suspiciously dirty; grit will never dissolve in food – we remember those disappointing cockles eaten at beachside kiosks! Remove the earthy root part of the stalk, and trim off any parts that look too damaged by greedy slugs, etc.

You can add some field mushrooms if you haven't managed to collect, find or purchase many. Slice them finely.

Sauté the rice and onion in the olive oil for about 3 minutes over a medium heat, until the rice is transparent but not sticking to the pan, and without browning the onion (it should be light gold and shiny). Then add the butter and garlic, and sauté the mushrooms for another couple of minutes. The fungi will release some of their moisture and this should stop the mixture sticking.

Now add the wine and stock and lightly season with salt and pepper (don't overdo it as you may want to adjust it later).

Cook the rice, stirring frequently for about 15–20 minutes, checking closely for softness. Risotto should have a fluid consistency, without being soupy, and have a bite to the centre of the rice. Overcook the rice and the dish will turn to porridge – so be careful! Near the end of the cooking time, add the cream and Parmesan, stirring in well. Adjust flavour using the stock and seasoning.

Serve in bowls, sprinkling over the top shavings of fresh Parmesan, a grind of pepper, a little chopped parsley and a few shavings of white Alba truffle.

* You can make an extra-flavoursome stock using light chicken stock with added dried mushrooms, such as ceps (*porcini*, in Italian). Simply pour the hot chicken stock over the fungi, and allow them to reconstitute for 2 hours until soft. Then squeeze the fungi dry to extract the last drops of flavour, and reserve the stock to add to the risotto later.

LOBSTER RAVIOLI IN SEAFOOD BROTH
WITH SAFFRON

BAKED TRANCHE OF TURBOT WITH
ROASTED FENNEL, SPINACH BURGER AND
GREEN HERB SAUCE

RIB-EYE OF VEAL AND FRENCH FRIES,
WITH DEEP-FRIED FRESH HERBS

SPAGHETTI WITH CUTTLEFISH AND PEAS

ORIENTAL FIREKETTLE SUPPER

SALAD OF GRILLED CRAYFISH WITH
OYSTER FRITTERS AND LEMON DRESSING

Mains for all Seasons

Living in a temperate climate, we are lucky to experience seasonal foods at their best, whether vegetables, fruits, fish or meat.

Advances in food distribution have increased accessibility to the gourmet experience of variety in diet. But it's both a blessing and a curse. Mass-market agriculture has been great for the farming economy, but disastrous for the gourmet. Huge quantities of mediocre vegetables and fruit may now be available all year round, but who relishes Spanish mass-farmed asparagus with the rapture usually reserved for the first crop of English or French varieties? You can get strawberries almost all the year round now, from far-flung places such as Chile . . . yet despite their bulk, they are all too disappointing on the tongue. It's hard to fight market forces – the odds seem against us. But are they?

During the 70s a small band of dedicated drinkers decided to make a stand against the appalling mediocrity that had crept into pub beers, and the Campaign for Real Ale took off. They never altogether demolished the big breweries' control but they did create an awareness that forced brewers to recognize the consumers' demands – and cater for them. Keg beer hasn't gone away, but at least real ale has a berth alongside.

We'll probably never get rid of mediocre-flavoured Dutch peppers, Iceberg lettuce or cardboard French apples, but let's hope there is some light at the end of the tunnel for the dedicated gourmandizer.

But don't despair. Advances are being made all the time. To take the example of brewing: the microbreweries that have sprung up in the last half of the decade have added weight and calibre to the dull offerings industrially produced, chasing the consumer hard and so forcing the big giants to think hard about the quality of their competition's brew.

With foods, supermarkets are trying to take the matter in hand by offering tomatoes 'on the vine', although we sometimes suspect that they are only charging higher prices for the same fruits that they've not bothered to pick properly. It is still an uphill struggle.

The one ray of hope? The Greenhouse Effect. A forward-looking gentleman at the Meteorological Office was noted for recently clearing land for olive groves in the Midlands. It prompts the question whether he knows something we don't. They say it's an ill wind that blows nobody any good, so let's pray for the day when we can drink a decent British merlot and discuss the merits of Newcastle versus Newbury for the best olives. Meanwhile, until we can throw away our greenhouses, we'll try to console you with some dishes for main courses that we have liked and loved over the years.

Lobster ravioli in seafood broth with saffron

SERVES 4

Ravioli has a strange heritage. Traditionally from the eastern seaboard of Italy, its name derives from the mariners' fare of *rabioli*, literally 'rubbish' – leftovers. Any suitable meat, fish or vegetable would be wrapped up in the pasta 'cushion' and cooked accordingly. Pasta dough is one of those things that are easy and quick to make yourself, yet the public perception is that it is too hard to bother with. Like anything, practice makes perfect, and pasta that you have made yourself, like bread, tastes all the more wonderful for that little extra effort.

Pasta has long been embraced by the British as both tasty and substantial, and generations have thrived on it. Here's a decidedly upmarket and luxurious new variety that Mr Heinz couldn't get into his original 57.

FISH STOCK
2.3 kg mixed fish bones, salmon heads etc.
1 large Spanish onion, peeled and halved
4 carrots
1 fennel bulb, halved (with the feathery tops)
1.75 litres water
4 black peppercorns
1 bottle light, dry white wine
225 g mushrooms (with stalks and peelings)
1 bouquet garni (bay leaf, parsley stalks, chervil)

SEAFOOD BROTH
2 tbsp olive oil
4 spring onions
2 cloves garlic, peeled and finely sliced
½ small red chilli, deseeded and finely chopped
6 mussels
6 clams
6 langoustines, cooked, the meat chopped and the shells reserved separately
4 beefsteak tomatoes, skinned and diced
a large pinch of saffron strands
150 ml dry Martini

PASTA
255 g pasta flour (durum or hard wheat, unbleached), sifted with 1½ tsp salt
3 eggs, beaten
2 tbsp olive oil
1 tsp saffron strands soaked in 2 tbsp hot water for 5 minutes

ROUILLE
4 tbsp fresh mayonnaise (see page 40)
3 hardboiled egg yolks, mashed
2 cloves garlic, pulped
a generous pinch of cayenne pepper

RAVIOLI
60 g shallots, chopped
1 tsp unsalted butter
240 g lobster, lightly cooked and diced
meat of 6 langoustines (reserved from above)

1 tbsp chopped fennel tops or dill
Maldon sea salt and freshly ground black pepper

TO SERVE
a handful of fresh chervil leaves

Fish stock method

Just about any fish are suitable for stock, so long as you don't just use too much oily fish (such as mackerel or tuna). Salmon heads are usually in plentiful supply at any time of year and flatfish give good flavours, being proportionately more skeleton than flesh. The only advice here is to ensure you remove any gills with stout scissors, since these sometimes give a bitter flavour to the stock – fiddly, but worth the effort!

Put all the ingredients in your largest pot, and bring to the boil. Skim off and discard any scum or froth. Lower the heat to a slow simmer, and cook for about 45 minutes, continuing to skim. Longer than this isn't really needed, unlike the meat stocks. Strain the liquid through a fine metal sieve or muslin then return it to the saucepan and reduce it by at least a quarter on a fast boil, so you end up with at least 1.7 litres of well-flavoured stock.

Tip: you can make this beforehand and keep it chilled for up to three days in the fridge or three months in the deep freeze (in a plastic container).

Seafood broth method

Heat the olive oil in a large saucepan over a moderate flame and sweat the spring onions until soft. Add the garlic, chilli, mussels, clams, langoustine shells, tomatoes, saffron, dry Martini, and fish stock, reduce the heat to low and simmer for 25 minutes until the shellfish are open and well cooked. Strain twice through a muslin-lined fine sieve. Discard the sieved material and reserve the broth.

Pasta method

Place the flour and salt, eggs, oil and saffron in the bowl of a food processor or mixer, and process together using the bread dough-hook or by hand, kneading it until it forms a soft dough.

If you're using a pasta-rolling machine, divide the dough into six pieces, then follow the manufacturer's instructions and feed them through the rollers. Adjust the thickness control to achieve a thin sheet; don't pull the sheets through, otherwise they will tear and shred. If you're rolling out by hand, divide the dough into three pieces. On a floured board roll each one out to the thickness of a small coin, then fold into three and roll slightly thinner. Repeat this about 6 times making the dough thinner each time. (Remember to keep the remainder of the dough covered whilst rolling each piece.)

Lay the finished sheets of pasta on a clean floured tea towel; don't overlap them, or they will stick together. If the sheets dry slightly, this is helpful to the 'handling' process. Dry polenta or semolina flour sprinkled over will help to ensure no sticking.

To make raviolis by hand, you can use a pastry cutting wheel or simply use a scone cutter to make a round form.

Rouille method

Combine all the ingredients together and reserve. Rouille is traditionally served on toasted baguette rounds and floated in the soup with a sprinkling of grated Gruyère or Parmesan on top. In this recipe we are using it as a binding for the ravioli contents.

Ravioli method

In a frying pan on a low to medium heat sweat the shallots in the butter and when soft remove the pan from the heat and add the lobster, langoustines, and fennel tops or dill. Mix well with the rouille and season.

Cut the ravioli into 7.5 cm squares, and place a tablespoon of the shellfish mixture in half of them. Paint the other squares with beaten egg. Cover each square with its top, egg side down, pressing down around each pile of filling to remove any air, then press each edge with the back of a stout knife to seal it.

Assembly

Reheat the broth. Boil the ravioli in plenty of well-salted boiling water for 3–4 minutes, remove carefully to prevent tearing at the edges, drain and place in warmed soup bowls. Pour the broth over, and finish with a scattering of chervil.

Baked tranche of turbot with roasted fennel, spinach burger and green herb sauce

SERVES 2

We are lucky to have available around our southwestern shores some excellent species of deep-water fish such as halibut and turbot. Turbots are generally caught 2 kg in weight and upwards. They are a large flatfish, similar to flounder and halibut, and fetch a high price, similar to wild salmon or line-caught halibut. They are superb and are well worth the expense. The wing tranche has a bone system similar to that of a skate and is easy to eat.

Fish is often accompanied by a simple covering of melted butter with parsley, or occasionally a warm hollandaise sauce. Here we adopt a more robust accompaniment taken from the strong traditions of Spain, Portugal and Italy.

2 × 350g pieces of fresh turbot wing
2 tbsp olive oil
Maldon sea salt and freshly ground white pepper
1 fennel bulb, trimmed, feathery tops reserved
2 tsp fennel seeds
240g fresh young leaf spinach, destemmed
freshly ground black pepper
60g unsalted butter
½ tsp freshly grated nutmeg
juice of ½ a lemon

TO SERVE
freshly chopped chervil
2 tbsp green herb sauce (see page 87)

Method

Trim the pieces of turbot free of fine fins and edge bones and any loose flaps of skin. Wash under cold running water, rubbing the skin free of any gunk. Pat dry with a tea towel. Now, with your fingers, rub each piece with ½ tbsp of the olive oil then season with salt and white pepper. Set aside and preheat the oven to 200°C/400°F/gas mark 6 while you prepare the vegetables.

Halve the fennel bulb. Remove and discard the V-shaped root and blanch the bulb for 3 minutes in boiling water with the fennel seeds and drain dry, then reserve both bulb and seeds to cool. Slice the bulb into narrow sections about 5mm thick. This will ensure they roast well along with the fish and will give a tender result that will still have some bite. Wash the spinach and leave to drain.

Place the fish pieces in the centre of a roasting tray with the blanched fennel around the edges. Season the fennel, coat it with the remaining olive oil

and dot it with half the butter, broken up with your fingertips into small pieces. Roast in the preheated oven for 20 minutes or so. (If it's fan assisted you may need to swing the tray around after 10 minutes or so and check that the fish is cooking evenly.)

After 10 minutes cook the spinach lightly for about 2–3 minutes in the water remaining on the leaves, turning it around to release the juices, then drain in a coarse sieve, pushing the juice out with a spoon. Season with salt, black pepper, and the nutmeg, add the remaining butter and mix it through. Now shape the spinach into two flat burger shapes which will form a base for serving the fish on. Keep warm ready for serving.

Finally, when the fish is cooked through, place each piece on a spinach burger. Squeeze the lemon over the fennel, and place around the fish on the plate. Sprinkle the chervil over it. Spread a spoonful of the herb sauce around one side, and a grind of black pepper will complete this superb dish.

Green herb sauce

The great dips and salsas of the Mediterranean – aïolis, pesto and anchoïades – call for a pestle and mortar. Pounding the ingredients in this time-honoured way seems to impart a more intense texture and character than simply using a blender to blitz the mixture. Oriental delis and supermarkets often have very robust granite pestle and mortars from Thailand, and these are ideal. Ensure the stone is clean and odour-free. If in doubt, after washing out, clean the inside surface with a cut half of lemon. This will guarantee an untainted surface.

1 clove garlic, peeled and finely chopped
3 tinned anchovy fillets, drained of oil,
*   roughly chopped*
1 tsp Dijon mustard
1 tbsp small capers, drained
30g flat-leafed parsley leaves
4 tbsp chopped coriander leaves
4 tbsp chopped basil leaves
feathery tops of the fennel, chopped
120ml virgin olive oil
Maldon sea salt and freshly ground black pepper
1 tsp lemon juice (to taste)

Method

Crush the garlic, anchovies, mustard and capers to a stiff paste. Add the herbs and fennel tops and continue pounding, adding oil every so often until smooth but with some grainy texture. Then season with salt, pepper and lemon juice.

Rib-eye of veal and French fries, with deep-fried fresh herbs

SERVES 2

Another simple dish inspired by a visit to New York. We ate a magnificent dinner on Madison which was memorable not only for the gigantic rib-eye steak on the bone, but for the fact that the chef insisted on coming out personally to advise us of his recommendations before each course! Whilst loving the attention, it felt a little pretentious to monopolize the head chef all evening so we opted instead to while away the time between courses smoking Lucky Strikes. The restaurant was so well-heeled and polite, it was well into dessert before the female maître d' plucked up the courage to ask us to desist. New Yorkers are so well drilled in the etiquette of not smoking in public places that it is rare for diners to have to be specifically asked. We avoided pleading tourist ignorance, unreservedly apologized to all around our table and were immediately forgiven. Largesse in New York is not confined to the portions.

2 ribs of veal*
2 tbsp olive oil
2 cloves garlic, peeled and crushed
Maldon sea salt and freshly ground white
  pepper
700g Desirée potatoes
sunflower oil for deep-frying

4 sprigs fresh thyme
large handful fresh basil leaves
4 large sprigs fresh watercress, leaves only
1 large bunch flat-leafed parsley, leaves only
1 sprig fresh rosemary
2 sprigs chervil, leaves only

Method

You will need a griddle pan with a ribbed surface.

Preheat the oven to 200°C/400°F/gas mark 6. Rub the meat surfaces with the olive oil and crushed garlic and season with salt and white pepper. Leave for 30 minutes at room temperature to allow the flesh to warm up.

Peel and slice the potatoes into long French-fry sized chips. Soak them in cold water, to help remove excess starch, then drain and dry thoroughly on a clean tea towel. Deep fry at 160°C/325°F for 2–3 minutes to cook the potato through. Drain well in the fryer basket and then tip out onto strong kitchen paper to drain, spreading the fries out well so they do not crush each other and go soggy.

To cook the meat, heat the griddle pan up to smoking hot and seal each side of the steaks for 2 minutes, moving the meat

once only through 45° so the markings crisscross each other (which looks very professional). Then, keeping both steaks on the hot griddle, place it into the hot oven until the meat is done: medium-rare should take no longer than 5 minutes.

While the veal is in the oven heat up the deep-frying oil to 180°C/350°F to finish the chips. Then mix a generous handful of fresh herbs into each basket of chips. Flash-fry each basket for about 1½–2 minutes until the fries are crisp and golden brown. The potato cools the oil as it fries so for maximum crispness only cook a small handful at a time. The herbs flavour the fries magnificently and can be eaten; discard the woody rosemary stems.

This indulgent meal only needs mustards for the steaks or mayonnaise for the fries to be complete. Additional vegetables would be a travesty here.

* Although beef on the bone was banned in the UK from New Year 1998, veal on the bone (under thirty months) is legal, so we have adapted this dish (under protest!) to current regulations. Traditionally, rib joints are cut with the rib-bone being sawn through in half longitudinally, but here ask your butcher to keep the whole rib intact. The resulting steak, will, therefore, beabout 4–5cm thick, with the bone whole and protruding about 18–20cm beyond the meat like a large handle. If you are lucky enough to live in a country without hampering regulations, enjoy this dish with mature beef!

Spaghetti with cuttlefish and peas

SERVES 4

Mick stole the idea for this recipe from an Italian restaurant in Sydney, and despite its boring name it tastes fantastic. You may think 'I can't eat cuttlefish, that's what you stick through the bars of a budgie cage', and of course, if you ate the backbone, you'd be right. However, in its fresh state, cuttlefish flesh tastes very good indeed, providing you follow the following recipe.

6 tbsp olive oil
6 small cuttlefish, cleaned and thinly sliced
  (see page 77)
4 cloves garlic, peeled
6 spring onions, chopped
300ml white wine
450g fresh petits pois
Maldon sea salt and freshly ground black pepper
a handful of chopped parsley
300ml tomato and basil sauce (see page 75)
250–400g spaghetti
60g unsalted butter

Method

You may have to make this dish in 2 batches. In a large frying pan, heat the oil and fry the cuttlefish with the garlic and spring onion for a few minutes without browning. Then discard the garlic and deglaze the mixture with the white wine. Add the peas and cook for a few minutes. Now add salt and pepper, the parsley and the tomato and basil sauce, and simmer for 5 minutes until the peas are done.

Cook the spaghetti in salted fast-boiling water until al dente. Drain, toss in the butter to prevent the strands sticking and then add to the cuttlefish mixture and combine thoroughly. Serve with freshly ground black pepper – traditionally, pasta dishes with fish do not have grated Parmesan on top.

Oriental firekettle supper

SERVES 4

The oriental firekettle encourages a communal type of eating where guests cook food in a central pot, rather like fondue. The difference is that instead of melting cheese they cook fish and meats on skewers in simmering stock. Then when all the slices of meats and fish have been eaten, a selection of vegetables is added to the stock and the resulting soup slurped as a final course. This method of cooking is sometimes called 'steamboat' and is always popular, if only for its novelty. Steamboat pots are available from large Chinese or Thai suppliers and you will need some charcoal to heat the central pipe of the kettle. It's also a good meal for doing outdoors. The secret of getting succulent bites is not to skimp on the quality of the fish and meats used.

In other parts of this book there are numerous recipes for dips and sauces suitable for oriental food. Feel free to experiment with them as additional dips to accompany this feast, but in our opinion, it is not necessary.

SOUP POT
900ml strong chicken stock (see page 57)
1 tsp finely grated fresh root ginger
1 clove garlic, peeled and crushed
8 quail's eggs, lightly boiled and shelled
30g fresh beansprouts
2 spring onions, cut into large pieces
120g raw king prawns, heads off
8 small spinach leaves
a dash of dark soy sauce
a small dash of hot pepper sauce
4 large sprigs chopped coriander, leaves and
 stems

SKEWERS

16 giant prawns
16 thin slices Scotch fillet beef
16 slices squid (including tentacles)
16 thin slices pork fillet
16 thin slices firm white fish (e.g. halibut)
16 thin slices fresh salmon fillet
16 small slices calf's liver
16 large scallops

Method

Place a fireproof mat under the base of the steamboat. Light the charcoal in the middle of the central flue. Heat the stock in a saucepan to just under the boil and decant into the steamboat reservoir. Add the ginger and garlic. (The other soup pot ingredients will be added later.)

Arrange the slices of meat and fish with the shellfish on individual platters with forked skewers. Guests can dine by spearing the titbit of their choice and simmering in the hot soup stock for a few minutes until done. Then they can consume them with gusto. Allow about 4 pieces of each type of flesh as per the ingredients list, so each diner has a substantial amount of protein by the end of Round One.

When all the guests have finished, add the soup pot ingredients to the stock and simmer for 1 minute to cook the shellfish and wilt the spinach, then ladle the soup into bowls for Round Two! (Chinese spoons and chopsticks lend authenticity here.)

This is a surprisingly filling meal (deceptive because one eats small slivers of food slowly), but it's a perfect style for creating that banquet feel while, because of the communal dipping into the soup, retaining a great informal atmosphere.

Salad of grilled crayfish with oyster fritters and lemon dressing

SERVES 6

Crayfish is probably Mick's favourite food. Given a choice of foods, this would be his desert island dish. Forget the complete works of Shakespeare and the Bible – pass the mayonnaise.

6 × 1kg fresh diver-caught Scottish crayfish
Maldon sea salt
2 tbsp olive oil
freshly ground black pepper
3 dozen oysters (Belon No. 2 are good)

4 tbsp seasoned plain flour
2 eggs, beaten
6 tbsp dried white breadcrumbs
sunflower oil for deep frying
mixed gourmet salad leaves, cleaned and
    trimmed (e.g. jaba, mizuna, tatsai, gold
    orach, red escarole, pea shoots, etc.)
a good handful (60g) sprouted onion seeds
1 × 350g jar keta (salmon caviar)

LEMON DRESSING
½ tsp Maldon sea salt
1 tbsp lemon juice
freshly ground black pepper
3 tbsp extra-virgin olive oil

Crayfish method

Cook each crayfish in boiling highly salted water (to mimic sea water) for 4–5 minutes and leave to cool.

Split each shell case lengthways, detach the tail meat and brush lightly with the olive oil and then season with salt and pepper.

Grill (ideally chargrill) each tail-meat piece for about 1 minute each side just before assembling the salad.

Oyster method

Shell the oysters, discarding the juices. Roll each mollusc in the flour, dip into the beaten egg and then roll until dry in fine breadcrumbs. Deep fry in hot oil (180°C/350°F) for about 30 seconds until the crumb coating is lightly coloured and then drain well on kitchen paper.

Lemon dressing method

Dissolve the salt in the lemon juice, add the pepper, whisk all ingredients together and adjust the seasoning.

Assembly

Just before serving, lightly dress the salad leaves with most of the lemon dressing, pile them in a neat cone on each plate and surround them with six beds of sprouted onion seeds. Place 2 halves of grilled crayfish tailmeat on the top of the pile and place an oyster fritter on each onion-seed bed. Garnish the crayfish with a tablespoon of keta and spoon a dash of lemon dressing over the top.

INDIAN FEAST

JAPANESE FEAST

OTTOMAN FEAST

CHINESE FEAST

PACIFIC FEAST

A World of Indulgence

Once upon a time, fine British cooking meant lavishness: Victorian banquet tables positively heaved under a wealth of dishes. Since those heady days, however, our repertoire has diminished into a meat-and-two-veg effort, the meagre shadow of a glorious heritage. But in the finest cuisines abroad there has been no such shrinkage, and when indulging in fine exotic restaurant food we still pamper ourselves like lords, accompanying succulent mains with lots of side dishes. Indeed, many foreign cooking styles lend themselves to a vast spread. Here we have recreated this sense of scale, grouping dishes together with their natural accompaniments as 'Feasts'.

The Chinese Feast favours old favourites, usually with easily found ingredients. For an ethnically correct accompanying flavour, try a beer like Shanghai's Zsing Tao. The Japanese Feast is a godsend to those with larger taste buds than wallets. For years raw fish purveyors have charged extortionate amounts for very small slivers, but we've unearthed their secrets, so you can make some of the most succulent food in the world easily yourselves at home. You can also find further recipes within this book. For instance, the Indian Feast will be washed down most excellently with Lassi (page 164), a sweet yoghurt drink whose sourish taste perfectly balances the hot, fiery subcontinental spicing.

We hope that the feasts, and the range of dishes themselves (any of which we encourage you to make by themselves, of course), will bring back some of the indulgence you revelled in on your holiday, yet without having to speak the language, set foot in a dodgy airport or suffer a bumpy road. *Bon appetit!*

Indian Feast

MARINATED KING PRAWNS
WITH TOMATO, CHARGRILLED CHILLI
AND CORIANDER SALSA

NOSH STUFFED NAAN

MINT AND CUCUMBER RAITA

'EMPEROR' CHICKEN TIKKA CURRY WITH
ALMONDS AND BASMATI RICE

SPICED LEMON DHAL

Marinated king prawns with tomato, chargrilled chilli and coriander salsa

SERVES 4

This is a perfect accompaniment for a rich course like Emperor curry (see page 101), strong on flavour but still leaving some room for later! You can buy boxes of uncooked green prawns at your fishmonger which are large enough to make the dreary task of shelling them less onerous. Appropriately enough, good prawns come from the Goa region.

16 large green prawns
2 tsp coriander seeds
a few fenugreek seeds
1 tsp mustard seeds
2 cloves garlic, peeled and thinly sliced
½ bunch chopped stems of coriander
1 tsp grated fresh root ginger
1 tsp paprika
a pinch of turmeric powder
juice of 3 limes
Maldon sea salt
peanut oil

CHILLI SALSA
1 red pepper
4 red chillies
2 tomatoes, skinned, deseeded and finely diced
juice of 2 limes
1 tsp olive oil
1 tsp palm sugar
½ small red onion, peeled and finely diced
1 bunch fresh coriander, leaves only
Maldon sea salt

Method

Peel the prawns and keep the small tail piece, discarding the head. Blitz the seeds, herbs and spices in the lime juice and marinate the prawns in this for 1–2 hours.

Meanwhile, char the red pepper and chillis by roasting over a flame or in a very hot oven (250°C/475°F/gas mark 9) for 10 minutes or so. Cool in a clingfilm-covered bowl. Skin them, deseed, and chop the flesh into small dice. Mix with the remaining salsa ingredients and rest for 1 hour in the fridge to let the flavours mingle.

To cook the prawns, drain and salt them and fry in a little peanut oil over a hot flame for a few minutes on both sides until they colour up pinky red. When cooked, spoon 2 tbsp of the marinade over them in the pan to deglaze them, then remove from the heat. Decant the shellfish onto plates for serving with a couple of spoonfuls of chilli salsa over them.

Nosh stuffed naan

450g plain flour, sifted
½ tsp Maldon sea salt
1 tsp baking powder
2 tsp caster sugar
2 tsp easy-blend dried yeast
1 large or 2 small eggs, beaten (at room
    temperature)
150ml plain or low-fat yoghurt (at room
    temperature)
150ml lukewarm whole milk

FILLING

2 tsp caster sugar
3 tbsp freshly grated coconut
3 tbsp ground almonds

TOPPING

60 ml clarified butter (see page 100)
1 tsp black onion seeds
2 tsp aniseeds
3 tsp crushed pistachio nuts

Method

Create the bread mix by sifting into a large bowl the flour, salt, baking powder, and sugar together with the dried yeast. Make a well in the centre, and add the egg, yoghurt and milk. Mix well together to form a dough and knead it on a floured work surface for about 10 minutes until it forms an elastic shiny ball. Sprinkle the ball with flour and place back into the bowl; clingfilm the bowl and set aside in a warm, draught-free place for about 1 hour, or until the dough has doubled in size.

Now preheat the oven to the highest temperature (250°C/475°F/gas mark 9) and place your heaviest based baking tray in it to preheat. If possible, also preheat your grill to the highest setting.

Now divide the dough into 8 equal balls. Keep them covered with a clean tea towel while you work on each one in turn.

Make each ball of dough into a tear shape, about 20cm long and about 10cm at the widest point.

To make the filling, place the sugar, almonds and grated coconut into a blender and process until the coconut has no gritty texture and the mix has become a soft paste. Cut a slot into one side of each naan and spread a little paste into the middle using a palette knife or similar.

Brush the top lightly with clarified butter and sprinkle some of the onion seeds, aniseeds and pistachios on top. Then place immediately on the hot baking tray in the hottest part of the oven for 3 minutes (it will puff up), then under the hottest part of the grill for 30 seconds or so just to brown slightly the naans on top. Wrap the finished naan breads in foil to keep warm and serve hot with curry.

Clarified butter

Clarified butter, or ghee, is a traditional cooking medium in many Indian dishes. Here it gives a smooth nutty taste to the finished naan bread. Although you can buy it from Indian stores it is easily made at home. Choose unsalted butter as there will be no salt to interfere with the seasonings of any recipe.

Gently melt 250g of butter in a heavy-based saucepan over a low flame. The milky residue will sink to the bottom. As the butter foams up, take it off the heat and let the particles subside. Strain the butter through muslin in a fine sieve, and pour into a sterile pot or jar. Keep in a cool place (a fridge is fine although well-made clarified butter will keep for a couple of weeks in a cold larder).

Mint and cucumber raita

SERVES 4

½ cucumber
575 ml low-fat live plain yoghurt
2 tbsp cold water
juice of ½ a lemon
Maldon sea salt and freshly ground black
 pepper
3 tbsp finely chopped mint
¼ tsp cayenne pepper
1 tsp cumin seeds, roasted

Method

The idea is to create a thin, sharp yoghurt dipping sauce and so it is one of the few times that we recommend a low-fat yoghurt. The sharpness cuts through the oil.

Peel and chop the cucumber into small cubes, discarding the seedy core, and mix into the yoghurt. Add the water, lemon juice, salt and pepper and mint, and stir around with a spoon a few times to let the flavours mingle. The consistency should be like single cream. Sprinkle with the cayenne and cumin.

'Emperor' chicken tikka curry with almonds and Basmati rice

SERVES 4

CHICKEN AND MARINADE
4 × 225g chicken supremes
3 tbsp plain yoghurt
1 tbsp red tandoori spice powder
1 tbsp tikka paste
juice of 1 lemon
2 tbsp sunflower oil
½ tsp Maldon sea salt

SAUCE
60g clarified butter (see page 100)
1 × 5cm piece fresh root ginger, finely shredded
3 cloves garlic, crushed
1 large onion
1 green pepper, deseeded, cored and diced
2 green chillis, deseeded and sliced into long
   thin strips
2 tbsp mild curry powder
½ tsp cardamom seeds (pods removed)
2 sticks cinnamon 'bark' (rolled leaf will do)
2 cloves
1 × 400ml can coconut milk
300ml tomato and basil sauce (see
   page 75)
juice of 1 lemon
Maldon sea salt and freshly ground black pepper
4 tbsp chopped fresh coriander leaves
about 6 tbsp ground almonds

TO SERVE
1 recipe basmati rice (see page 102)
single cream

flaked halved almonds, lightly toasted
coriander leaves

Grill method

Trim the chicken of skin, sinews and fat
and cut into large chunks (6 to 8 from
each supreme). Mix together the marinade
ingredients into a moist paste and coat
each chicken piece thoroughly in a bowl.
Cover and leave to marinate for a couple
of hours. (If left overnight, leave the salt
out until the next day, or the meat juices
will be extracted and the flesh will be
tough.)

Cook on a very hot grill (a chargrill
will give that authentic tandoori flavour).
Ensure the meat is not overdone – it will
be simmered in a sauce later. Grill it rare
to keep the juices intact, about 5 minutes
only.

Sauce method

In a heavy-based casserole, heat the clarified butter over a medium heat and sauté
the ginger, garlic, onion and pepper for a
few minutes, stirring around occasionally.
Then add the chillies and spices and cook
for another 3 minutes on a low heat. Pour

in the coconut milk, tomato and basil sauce and lemon juice, and season. Simmer on a low heat for 10 minutes or until the onion and peppers are soft, then add the grilled chicken pieces and simmer for another 3 minutes more. Add the coriander and then thicken the sauce with the ground almonds – adding gradually until the right consistency is reached. Too much and the sauce will be thick like wallpaper paste, too little and the sauce may be too thin and runny to cling to the meat.

Finally, adjust the seasoning. To serve – with plain boiled basmati rice – simply spoon over a little single cream, a sprinkling of flaked almonds and a few fresh coriander leaves for colour.

Basmati rice

.Rice is quite a simple thing to cook, but many people just can't get it right. Use basmati rice, the king of Indian rice, and wash it well in cold water. The water will be cloudy with the excess starch, and can be discarded. With each refill of fresh water, the cloudiness will diminish until the rice can be swirled around the bowl with the rinsing water remaining clear. This will take about ten rinses. You may regard this as particularly tedious, but it's essential for a good separation of the grains when cooked.

PER MEASURE (SAY A CUP MEASURE PER PERSON) OF RICE
2½ measures cold water
a few drops of lemon juice
a good pinch of Maldon sea salt
a hazelnut-sized knob of butter

Method

Place all the ingredients in a saucepan with a tightly fitting lid over a high heat. When the steam escapes from under the lid, indicating it has boiled, turn the heat down to very low, stir the rice once only, to turn the bottom rice to the top of the pile, and replace the lid. Cook very gently for about 8 minutes or so, tasting a few grains every so often. They should be soft but not soggy, al dente (just like pasta), and if they are still hard and gritty then another couple of minutes should do it.

Give it a final stir and take the rice off the heat, keeping the lid on to let it cook on in its own steam for a few minutes. Then take the lid off and let any excess steam escape for a couple of minutes more. This is essential so that you get grains that look dry to the eye, but are soft and moist to the palate.

Preferably, rice should be served as soon as possible after it is ready. Covered, it will keep hot and all right for a while, but don't expect it to last for hours. Rice will continue to cook on in its own heat and eventually the mass will thicken and solidify. If it must wait longer than 10 minutes you can keep it refreshed by steaming in a metal or wicker colander over barely boiling water. Avoid the temptation of running cold water over finished rice or stirring it around with a spoon too much, as cooked rice goes to a mush all too easily. Use a fork to gently fluff up the grains for serving.

Remember, there is no foolproof way to cook rice because there are so many different varieties and types. But most packaged rice indicates a guide for cooking times and with practice you should soon be able to estimate and deal with the small differences.

Spiced lemon dhal

SERVES 4–6

Dhal is a generic term for the range of Indian pulses that includes mung beans, peas, lentils and many others. The dishes may range in style from hot stews to spicy pastes and soups. This particular dhal is a spicy and sharp dish that has the consistency of porridge: it can be eaten with a fork, but is also liquid enough to dip your bread or naan into.

675g split red lentils
2 large carrots, peeled and finely diced
1 small onion, peeled and thinly sliced
4 curry leaves
1 tsp mild curry powder
2 tsp cumin seeds
1 tsp ground cumin
1 tsp ground coriander

½ tsp cardamom seeds (pods removed)
2 whole cardamom pods
3 cinnamon sticks (the darker bark is best)
3 cloves
2 bay leaves
1 tsp whole mustard seeds
½ tsp ground turmeric
60ml unsalted butter, clarified (see page 100)
4 tbsp sunflower oil
2 green chillies, deseeded, and thinly sliced lengthways
5 fat cloves garlic, peeled and thinly sliced into strands
1 tbsp grated fresh root ginger
2 tbsp chopped coriander (leaves and stems)
1 tsp garam masala
juice of 3 lemons
2 tsp Maldon sea salt

Indian Feast
103

Method

Wash the lentils, picking out any dark seeds or husks, and drain thoroughly, thenput them in a large pot with the carrots and the onion and about 1.2 litres of water, and bring to the boil. Remove any froth or scum that rises to the surface. Turn the heat down and simmer slowly with the lid slightly ajar for about 40 minutes, until the lentils are soft. Stir from time to time, and keep a check on the water level. You want to have a thick soupy consistency, not too watery. Add a dash or two of boiling water if it seems to be getting too dry.

Meanwhile, put the next twelve ingredients in a small saucepan with the clarified butter and oil, and sizzle over a medium heat for a few minutes, stirring, then add the chilli, garlic and ginger and continue to cook on a slightly lower heat until the garlic starts to slightly brown. Remember not to overcook the garlic as it will turn bitter.

The mustard seeds will now start to spit and burst, so pour the entire mix – oil and spices – into the lentil pot. Add the coriander and garam masala and mix together. Add the lemon juice. If you have an electric rotary hand-held whisk you can give the dhal a couple of quick whizzes around to liquefy part of the lentils – but don't purée them completely, it's best to have some degree of graininess for bite and texture. Taste, and adjust the seasoning. The dhal can be simmered on a very low heat for another 5 minutes, but don't forget to check the pot and stir to prevent any sticking or burning on the bottom.

Japanese Feast

TUNA 'KOBE' CARPACCIO WITH
SOY SAUCE, GINGER, WASABE
AND VIRGIN OLIVE OIL

SWORDFISH ON A BED OF SAMPHIRE

CRISPY DUCK 'HIROSHIMA' WITH
SPINACH AND SESAME SEEDS

VEGETABLE TEMPURA WITH
GARLIC SOY SAUCE DIP

SESAME AND GINGER DIPPING SAUCE

SPICY SEAFOOD AND CHICKEN RAMEN

DEEP-FRIED KING PRAWNS WITH
SWEET CHILLI JAM AND LIMES

Tuna 'Kobe' carpaccio with soy sauce, ginger, wasabe and virgin olive oil

SERVES 8

450g fresh yellowfin tuna in the piece*
4 tbsp virgin olive oil
2 tbsp finely shredded fresh root ginger
3 tsp wasabe (Japanese horseradish mustard)
3 tbsp soy sauce

Method

Although firm fleshed, fresh raw tuna is still hard to slice thinly and neatly. Use a mechanical slicer if you are fortunate enough to have that luxury, or place the fish, tightly wrapped in clingfilm, in the freezer for 20 minutes. This will firm the flesh enough to slice it thinly, like ham, with a very sharp blade.

Arrange 3 large slices on a plate, and pour over a trickle of olive oil. Add a small pile of ginger and a tiny dollop of wasabe (not too much, it's quite hot), at one side. Sprinkle a few drops of soy sauce over the oil.

With the soy sauce there should be no need to put salt on the fish.

* Yellowfin tuna is just one of various types of tuna. Most will do for this dish, but beware of using bonito tuna, which is a very bloody-fleshed fish and does not give a good result here.

Swordfish on a bed of samphire

SERVES 8

Swordfish benefits from being cooked fresh, and now airfreight distribution times are so rapidly reduced it is possible to eat deep-sea fish from exotic locations like Madagascar within a few days of it being caught. If you're buying swordfish from a supermarket fishmonger's counter, you should avoid any fish that have been frozen, as this radically affects the texture.

Samphire is a tidal sea plant native to British shores. Unfortunately, it is not cultivated as a gourmet delicacy and supplies have to be imported from France, or more recently the Persian Gulf.

Samphire is eaten raw or very lightly cooked, but needs picking through and washing well, to remove any chaff or woody bits (the stems near the anchor root get woody and inedible with time). Stir-fried

here with soy sauce, ginger and chilli, it is a feast for the taste buds. Do not overcook your samphire – it should retain some crunch.

8 × 240g steaks of swordfish loin (or 16 ×
*   120g pieces if the loin is at the tail end)*
5 tbsp olive oil
Maldon sea salt and freshly ground white pepper
1.3 kg samphire, cleaned and
*   picked through*
1 clove garlic, peeled and minced
1 small red chilli, deseeded and finely chopped
1 × 2.5cm piece root ginger, grated
a few drops of sesame oil
2 tbsp soy sauce
a small knob of unsalted butter
freshly ground black pepper

Method

Trim the fish steaks of any bony spines or fins, but leave the skin intact. Brush each piece with olive oil (use 2 tbsp) and season with salt and white pepper.

Pour the rest of the olive oil into a large frying pan on a medium–hot flame. While waiting for it to heat up wash the samphire stalks in lightly salted water and drain.

Pan-fry each steak for about 2–3 minutes each side and drain dry on kitchen towel. Keep warm while cooking the samphire.

Into a wok on a very high flame throw in the samphire and stir-fry for a few seconds in its own moisture with the garlic, chilli and ginger until heated through. Add the sesame oil and soy sauce. Continue to stir-fry for another couple of minutes, tossing continuously. Finish off by adding the butter and taking off the heat. Swirl the butter around the wok to give the samphire a shine. Using tongs, place portions on each warmed plate and arrange the fish neatly on top. Sprinkle with black pepper.

Crispy duck 'Hiroshima' with spinach and sesame seeds

SPICE MIX
1 tsp ground anise
¼ tsp garlic powder
½ tsp freshly ground white pepper
3 tbsp dark soy sauce
½ tsp ground ginger

½ tsp mild chilli powder
2 tsp soft brown sugar
a little Maldon sea salt

DUCK 'HIROSHIMA'
1 duck (no giblets)

NOSH BROTHERS' WORLD FAMOUS
HONEY DRESSING
a large pinch of Maldon sea salt
2 tbsp raspberry or cider vinegar
2 tbsp runny honey (a strong one is good)
4 tbsp virgin olive oil
freshly ground black pepper

SALAD
*900g baby spinach (pousse), washed and
    drained*
6 spring onions, chopped
120g baby cherry tomatoes
2 tbsp sesame seeds, toasted

Method

The initial part of the preparation can be done the day before to save time on the night.

First, stir all the spice mix ingredients together. Prick the skin of the duck all over with a fork then blanch it in boiling water for about 10 minutes. Drain dry, allow to cool, then rub the spice mix firmly into the duck skin and let it rest for at least 15 minutes.

Meanwhile, preheat the oven to 220°C/425°F/gas mark 7 and roast the bird for 25–35 minutes, or until the juices run clear when pricked with a skewer. This pricking and roasting will remove a good part of the fat lying just under the skin.

For the final part of the process, you need to deep-fry the bird in hot oil (200°C/400°F) to crisp the skin, about 3–4 minutes. When drained, the flesh, which has become drier, can be teased apart from the bones – rather like the consistency of the duck served in your local Chinese restaurant.

To make the dressing, dissolve the salt in the vinegar, stir in the honey, then add the oil and stir. Season with black pepper. Warm it through if you like, but very gently, otherwise it will split and the flavours evaporate.

Mix the spinach with the dressing, adding the spring onions and cherry tomatoes. Drape pieces of the crispy duck about the salad. (The duck meat is still quite rich and does not require any salad dressing on the flesh.) Top with a sprinkle of the sesame seeds.

Vegetable tempura with garlic soy sauce dip

SERVES 2

Mick first had tempura as a student. A flatmate had invited at short notice three passing Japanese students as houseguests. The larder cupboards were bare and

potential embarrassment loomed in the kitchen quarter. Peeking behind the green baize door, the visitors laughed and pointed out flour, soy sauce, a leek, and a carrot, which they claimed was a feast. Shredding the vegetables finely together and binding them with a batter, they deep-fried them and served them with a spicy dipping sauce made by mixing soy sauce and crushed garlic in a little boiling water.

It was both a delight and a revelation and a lesson that you don't need elaborate ingredients to make something tasty.

SOY SAUCE AND GARLIC DIP
4 tbsp soy sauce
2 tbsp mirin (Japanese rice wine)
1 garlic clove, finely chopped

TEMPURA
1 small aubergine
1 red pepper and 1 green pepper, cored, deseeded and cut into large dice

120g baby sweetcorn, blanched and halved
  lengthways
2 large spring onions, halved
peanut oil for deep-frying

BATTER
120g plain flour
1 egg yolk
175ml water
a few drops of sesame oil
a pinch of salt

Dip method

Warm all the ingredients together (do not boil) in a saucepan, and rest to allow the flavours to mingle. Warm gently for serving.

Tempura method

Slice the aubergine into 5mm discs, salt them well, and leave them to disgorge their bitter juice for say 1 hour, then rinse them and dry them well. All the ingredients should be dry.

Mix the batter ingredients together well and dip each piece of vegetable into it. Shake the excess off on the side of the bowl, and deep-fry for a couple of minutes in small batches. The oil should be quite hot (180°C/350°F) and the batches should be kept small, so that the oil does not cool down too much. Test the temperature of the oil first by placing a small cube of dry white bread into it. If it sizzles, the oil is hot enough. Too hot, i.e. smoking, and the batter will burn before the vegetables have time to cook through. Drain the batches on kitchen paper and keep warm until all are ready for serving.

Sesame and ginger dipping sauce

This alternative sauce to the soy sauce and garlic dip is easy to make.

2 tsp sesame oil
2 tbsp kecup manis (sweet soy sauce)
2 tbsp mirin (Japanese rice wine)

3 tbsp ginger syrup (from a stem ginger jar)
1 tbsp runny honey
2 spring onions, finely chopped

Simply mix all the liquids together and scatter the spring onions on top.

Spicy seafood and chicken ramen

Ramen is a generic term for a noodle dish that traditionally uses buckwheat noodles. We prefer to use udon noodles, fat white rice noodles that have a slightly softer, more luxurious texture. The choice is yours.

PER PERSON

¼ chicken breast

1 tbsp soy sauce

2 king prawns, cut in half along the centre

3 pieces of squid, about 6cm long each

1 scallop

4 mussels

4 seasonal green leaves (spinach, pea-shoots, pak choi, etc.)

100g udon noodles

Maldon sea salt

300ml strongly flavoured fish stock* (see page 84)

2 tbsp beansprouts

1 large crab claw, cooked, shelled, and thinly sliced

1 lobster tail, cooked, split in half, and shelled

1 × 2.5cm piece daikon, finely grated

1 × 5mm piece root ginger, finely grated

GARNISH

a few pieces of wakame or nori seaweed

2 spring onions, finely chopped

Method

Marinate the chicken breast in the soy sauce for 30 minutes then grill it until almost done. Slice thinly, ready for the topping.

Steam the king prawns, squid, scallop, mussels and seasonal green leaves for a few minutes without overcooking them.

Blanch the noodles in boiling salted water for a few minutes until soft but al dente and heat the fish stock to near boiling (do not actually boil the soup).

Arrange the drained noodles in the bowl, spread over all the remaining ingredients as toppings and arrange them neatly. Pour over the hot stock and then garnish with the seaweed and spring onion.

* To the fish stock add: a little mouli (oriental white radish), coriander leaves, watercress and a small amount of grated root ginger.

Deep-fried king prawns with sweet chilli jam and limes

PER PERSON
4 raw king prawns
cornflour, sifted (for dusting)
4 egg yolks, whisked with a little cold water
salt and freshly ground black pepper
dry white breadcrumbs for coating
peanut oil for deep frying
1 recipe sweet chilli jam (see below)
lime wedges

Method

Slice along the back of each prawn and remove the dark vein. Pat dry and dust with cornflour, shaking the excess off. Dip each prawn into the seasoned egg and coat with breadcrumbs. Deep-fry for a few minutes until fully cooked and cool quickly. Serve with the chilli jam and wedges of fresh lime to squeeze.

Sweet chilli jam

MAKES 350ML

1 large red chilli, deseeded and cored
4 large cloves garlic, peeled
100ml white wine vinegar
150g caster sugar
125g plum jam, sieved
1 tbsp cornflour

Method

Chop and blitz the chilli and garlic in a blender. Transfer to a saucepan and add the remaining ingredients. Bring to the boil and simmer until smooth, stirring frequently – about 5 minutes. Pass through a coarse sieve and cool before storing in a plastic container.

Ottoman Feast

KLEFTIKO WITH WARM POTATO
AND AUBERGINE SALAD

BABAGANOUSH

CALAMARI WITH FRESH TARTARE SAUCE

HUMMUS WITH HOME-BAKED
PITTA BREAD

Kleftiko with warm potato and aubergine salad

SERVES 6

Kleftiko is a leg (or shank) of lamb on the bone, marinated and roasted slowly to release all the juices from the meat into the pan. We have always been great fans of mutton, which although coarser-textured and fattier than lamb, has a flavour that is much underrated and is rather unfashionable. This is a perfect example of a recipe that would benefit from a fatty meat like mutton, keeping the joint moist right to serving.

In Greece, where marjoram − *rigani* − grows wild, the Greeks use the flowering tops. These have a strong, unique flavour and aroma (if you've been to the Greek islands you'll know that heavy aroma that hits you on a hot afternoon in the hills). If you are lucky enough to go to Greece, pick a few bunches of it wild. Dried, it will keep its scent for a few months. If you can't get it, Camisa in Old Compton Street, London W1 (0171 437 7610) has a supply of dried wild marjoram (oregano), better than the supermarkets' dried sweet marjoram. Ask for it − they keep it under the counter!

The cooking method for kleftiko is a variation of that called *sofrito* in Spain, a

combination of roasting and stewing in a little liquid.

1 leg of lamb
4 tbsp olive oil
2 large onions, coarsely sliced
Maldon sea salt and freshly ground black pepper
juice of 3 lemons
1 tbsp oregano
1 bunch chervil
4 cloves garlic, thinly sliced
250 ml dry white wine
450g tomatoes, skinned and cored

Method

Place the meat in a large roasting pan with the olive oil and onions and turn it over a hot flame to seal and brown it all over.

Agitate the onions gently so they do not burn. When the joint is brown, season it, paint it with lemon juice and herbs, sprinkle it with garlic, pour in the white wine and tomatoes and then cover with foil and cook slowly in a preheated oven at 160°C/325°F/gas mark 3 for 2–2½ hours until the meat is very tender and falling away from the bone (adjust the temperature as necessary to ensure the meat does not dry out). You will need to top up the liquid in the bottom of the pan with a little water from time to time (check every 25 minutes). The idea is that the meat is simmered very gently in its own juices, which are released by the salt, tomatoes and the heat, until a rich gravy is formed.

Serve with the following warm potato salad.

Warm potato and aubergine salad

450g small aubergines
Maldon sea salt
8 tbsp virgin olive oil
2 cloves garlic, peeled and sliced
350g old potatoes, parboiled, peeled and cut into large dice
juice of ½ a lemon
1 tsp caster sugar
6 spring onions, coarsely diced
350g tomatoes, peeled and quartered
3 tbsp chopped flat-leaf parsley
1 tbsp chopped coriander
freshly ground black pepper

Method

Cut the aubergines into 1cm discs and salt them well to remove any bitter juices. After 1 hour, rinse in plenty of cold water, drain well and pat dry with a clean dry tea towel. Sauté them lightly in the olive oil in a high-sided saucepan over a low to medium heat for about 15 minutes, turning frequently and adding the garlic after 10 minutes. Then add the potatoes, lemon juice, sugar, spring onions and tomatoes, mixing well together, and simmer for 30–45 minutes until the potatoes are soft and all the vegetables have cooked together (stir the dish after every 10 minutes and check the dish does not overcook). Then add the herbs and check the seasoning.

The idea of this dish is for the vegetables to be simmered together so that the flavours intermingle, yet the cooking should not be so fierce that the veg breaks down into a mush, which spoils it. It should be served while still warm and have a rich red colour and be shiny from the generous amount of virgin oil in the tomato sauce.

Babaganoush

SERVES 6

3 large aubergines
Maldon sea salt
4 cloves garlic, peeled and crushed
150g tahini (sesame seed paste)
juice of 3 lemons, to taste
1 tsp ground cumin
black pepper to taste

TO SERVE
1 tbsp virgin oil
1 tbsp toasted whole cumin seeds
1 tbsp finely chopped flat-leaf parsley
a few black Kalamata olives
pitta breads

Method

Roast the aubergines either in a very hot oven (230°C/450°F/gas mark 8) or in a kettle barbecue with the lid on for about 15 minutes or so until the skins blister and peel off. Peel and wash them and squeeze out any bitter juices.

Pound some salt to taste with the garlic and add the aubergine flesh, mashing with a fork (do not blitz as this spoils the texture). Add the tahini and lemon juice and then the cumin and pepper.

Keep adjusting the mix until it is a proper blend of rich tahini, smoky aubergine and sharp lemon.

Pour the aubergine mixture into a bowl or shallow platter, and garnish with a drizzle of olive oil, the cumin seeds, parsley and a scattering of olives. To eat, dip toasted pitta soldiers into the paste, and enjoy!

Calamari with fresh tartare sauce

Squid (calamari), like mussels, are quite underrated and very inexpensive. They are a bit messier to clean but pay dividends in the flavour department. Don't be tempted *under any circumstances* to use frozen squid. Freezing renders them tough and quite horrible. In fact, many people who say they don't like squid are quite converted once they eat fresh ones. Small squid are much more delicate in texture, so the secret here is not to buy the big rubbery ones that seem good value (or easier to clean).

PER PORTION
*3 small squids, cleaned**
seasoned flour for dredging (mixed 3:1 plain flour to polenta)
Maldon sea salt and freshly ground black pepper
peanut or sunflower oil for deep-frying

TO SERVE
chervil, finely chopped
lemon wedges
Tartare sauce (see below)

Method

Cut each squid body into ring sections and the tentacles into lengths. Dust generously with the seasoned flour dredge, and deep-fry in hot oil (180°C/350°F) in a wire basket for a few minutes until the coating is crisp. When cooked through, drain on kitchen paper and sprinkle with sea salt and chervil and serve with wedges of fresh lemons and the tartare sauce.

It is possible to shallow-fry the squids in olive oil, but the high temperature of the peanut oil ensures a much crisper result.

* To clean squid, first take off the outer purply/pink skin and discard it. Now gut the squid, cut off the head above the eyes but retain the tentacles. Remove the clear 'plastic' inner bone (actually cartilage) and wash the body free of grit.

Tartare sauce

SERVES 6–8

1 tbsp dill vinegar (from the gherkins)
juice of ½ a lemon
150ml thick fresh mayonnaise (see page 40)
60g large pickled capers
4 spring onions, finely chopped
3 large dill-pickled sweet and sour gherkins, finely chopped
1 tbsp chopped chervil or dill

Method

Add the liquids to the mayonnaise and fold in the other ingredients. Chill in the fridge for an hour for the flavours to blend. Add a generous dollop to each plate to dip the calamari into.

Hummus with home-baked pitta bread

SERVES 4

Hummus is a famous spicy chickpea paste and is still one of the best-known elements of Middle Eastern cooking. Each country has its own version, whether it's Iran, Turkey, Greece or the Lebanon. We favour the Israeli version here, served with a hot dressing of chickpeas in broth.

If you are lucky enough to know your way around the Jewish deli territory of Golders Green in North London you can find wonderful freshly baked pitta breads. But try making your own. With some pitta this hot starter, if in a generous enough portion, is fine for a snack meal on its own.

240g dried chickpeas
1.1 litres chicken stock (see page 34)
2 cloves garlic, peeled and crushed
1 tbsp tahini (sesame seed paste)
2 tsp ground cumin
5 tbsp virgin olive oil
juice of 1 lemon
a pinch of cayenne pepper
Maldon sea salt

1 tsp cumin seeds, toasted
a dash of virgin olive oil
2 tbsp chopped flat-leaf parsley
Pitta bread (see below)

Method

Cover the chickpeas with boiling water and leave to soak overnight. Next morning, drain them and cook in the chicken stock for 1–1½ hours or until tender (this depends on the age of the chickpeas). Drain, reserving the cooking liquid and 60g of the cooked whole chickpeas (for the garnish). When cooled slightly, pulse the cooked chickpeas with the garlic in a blender (do not overprocess – try to keep a coarse texture to give the purée some bite). Add the tahini, cumin, olive oil and lemon juice. Check the seasoning, adding cayenne pepper and salt to taste, and if required add some cooking liquor to loosen the consistency.

To serve, spoon a ladle of hummus into a shallow bowl, pressing it around the sides of the bowl. Combine a couple of spoonfuls of the broth with the reserved chickpeas. Sprinkle the hummus with the cumin seeds, olive oil, and parsley, and pour the chickpea/broth mixture in the middle. Eat with warm pitta bread.

Pitta bread

MAKES ABOUT 6–8 LARGE PITTA BREADS

Everyone knows the distinctive flat oval of pitta bread that accompanies most Middle Eastern starters. This flat disc with all the appeal of a savoury beermat bears no relation to the aromatic pockets of pittas baked on a metal dome over an open charcoal fire. Realistically, we cannot reproduce this at home, so we'll have to make do with a domestic oven. But the effort is well worth it, especially when in pursuit of the grail of indulgence rather than merely 'filling a gap'.

Pieces of bread can be broken off and used to envelop a tasty morsel of meat or scoop up some hummus or Baba- ganoush. When one is in a hurry, split it in two and stuff it for a home-made take away. It's also without question the best way of mopping up the juices left on the plate at the end of a meal. Dispense with niceties, and dip yer bread in!

450g strong white bread flour
1 level tsp Maldon sea salt
1 sachet easy-blend dried yeast
300ml lukewarm water
3 tbsp olive oil

Method

Sift the flour, salt and yeast into a bowl and make a well in the centre. Add the water and oil to make a dough, and work it well on a floured board until it is smooth, shiny and elastic. 10–15 minutes should give a good result, but if you are lucky enough to have an electric mixer with a bread-dough hook, 5 minutes will be enough. Smear the dough with a little extra oil and let it rest in the bowl, in a warm place, covered with clingfilm, for 1–2 hours or until it has doubled in size.

Next, take a piece of risen dough the size of your fist and flatten it on a lightly floured surface first with your hand and then with a floured rolling pin until it is about 5mm thick. Dust with extra flour and lay on a floured tray in a warm place to rise again (to prove) for 30 minutes, and preheat your oven to maximum (at least 230°C/450°F/gas mark 8).

Place lightly oiled heavy-based baking trays in the oven for 5 minutes so the metal is very hot. Slip the flat rounds of dough onto them, and bake for about 10 minutes (without opening the oven door): as they bake the breads should puff up so that a natural pouch forms inside. Cool them on a wire rack.

They are best eaten fresh from the hot oven, but to reheat them simply toast in an electric toaster or wrap them in foil and put them in a warm oven for a few minutes.

A traditional seasoning for pitta breads is *zahtar* (pronounced 'sach-turr'). This is toasted sesame seeds, crushed with salt, a little dried thyme, and spices. It can be sprinkled over the breads as they come out of the oven or the bread can be dipped into it with olive oil as a condiment.

Chinese Feast

CUTTLEFISH CAKES WITH A RICE
VINEGAR AND CHILLI DRESSING

CANTONESE-STYLE ROAST DUCK WITH
CHINESE BROCCOLI, OYSTER SAUCE AND
CHOW MEIN NOODLES

WHOLE SEA BASS BAKED IN SALT

PRAWN, GINGER AND SPRING ONION DIM
SUM, WITH A SWEET AND SOUR DIP

PORK, SHRIMP AND
WATER CHESTNUT DIM SUM

Cuttlefish cakes with a rice vinegar and chilli dressing

PER PERSON
60g raw white fish, deboned and flaked
90g chopped cleaned cuttlefish (or squid)
30g cooked shelled prawns or shrimps,
    chopped
1 spring onion, finely chopped
1 tsp light soy sauce
½ tsp chilli sauce
a dash of whisked egg
a pinch of turmeric powder
½ garlic clove, peeled and crushed
1 tsp finely grated fresh root ginger
a few chopped coriander leaves
Maldon sea salt and freshly ground white pepper
plain flour for coating
peanut oil for shallow frying

TO SERVE
Rice vinegar and chilli dressing (see below)

Method

Blend all the ingredients except for the flour and oil roughly together in a food processor. Do not let it get too fine – it should have a coarse texture.

Shape into 4–5cm diameter cakes, then dip into the flour and shallow-fry in hot peanut oil for a few minutes on each side until golden brown, crisp on the outside and soft and moist in the middle. To serve, dip them into the dressing.

Rice vinegar and chilli dressing

2 cloves garlic, peeled and finely chopped
2 small red chillies, deseeded and chopped
½ tbsp shrimp paste*
1 tbsp Thai fish sauce
2 tbsp lemon juice
2 tbsp rice vinegar
2 tbsp caster sugar
a few chopped coriander leaves

Method

Blend all the ingredients thoroughly in a food processor for 3 minutes until well mixed.

* The shrimp paste can be obtained from all good oriental delis. Toast it lightly on a small square of kitchen foil before crumbling it into the dressing.

Cantonese-style roast duck with Chinese broccoli, oyster sauce and chow mein noodles

SERVES 4–6

We have all seen the ducks hanging in the windows of Cantonese restaurants, complete with neck, head, and feet (in China nothing is wasted). Most people order the crispy duck in Chinese restaurants. This is of course fine, especially in the indulgence stakes, but roast duck Cantonese style is often overlooked.

1 whole fresh duck
3 tbsp brandy
1 tbsp yellow bean paste
120 ml soy sauce
1 tbsp ground aniseed
2 tbsp runny honey

TO SERVE
raw shelled peanuts in their skins

Method

Ensure the inside cavity of the duck is free of giblets. Pour boiling water over the outside and inside the cavity of the bird. This will clean and loosen the skin. Drain the bird and pat dry with a cloth. Brush the skin with the brandy and hang up to dry. (A couple of hours will do it.) Some people go mad and use hair dryers . . . This part of the preparation can be done the day before.

Prick the skin all over with a fork. Mix together the yellow bean paste, soy sauce, aniseed and honey, and rub it firmly into the skin. Leave to rest for at least 15 minutes.

Meanwhile, preheat the oven to 220°C/425°F/gas mark 7 then roast the bird upside down for 25–30 minutes. Reduce the temperature to 190°C/375°F/ gas mark 5 and roast breast uppermost for another 45–55 minutes, or until the juices run clear when pricked with a skewer. This will remove a good part of the fats lying just under the skin itself. This method of roasting the duck is intended to give a fully cooked meat with little or no pinkness, but which has a moist consistency and no dryness. Add the peanuts 15 minutes before the end of cooking, and once roasted leave them in the juices to soften.

When roasted, take the bird out of the oven and drain the juices from the inner cavity. Skim off any fat left on the surface of the pan with a piece of kitchen towel and add the juices to the pan. Reduce these slightly by bubbling on the hob (with a couple of spoonfuls of chicken stock if the yield is too low). When the bird is carved spoon the hot gravy over it, along with the peanuts.

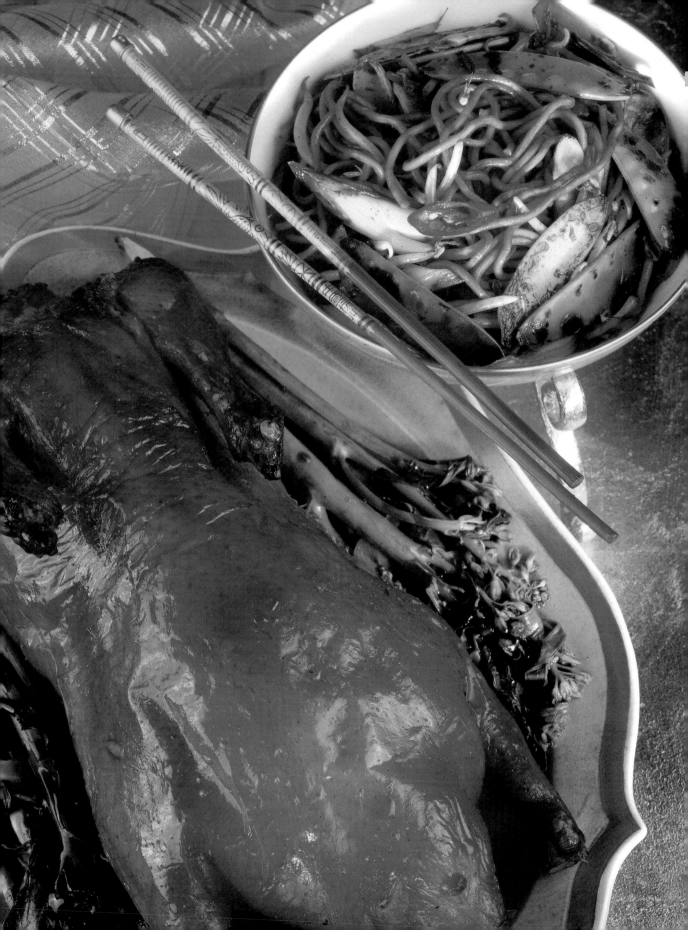

Chinese broccoli

PER PERSON
4 small stems Chinese broccoli
3 tbsp peanut oil
2 cloves garlic, peeled and thinly sliced
175 ml chicken stock (see page 57)
*3 tbsp bottled real oyster sauce**

Method

Trim the broccoli stems at the bottom, and remove any sprouting buds that have flowered.

Heat a wok until smoking, add the peanut oil and wilt the stems of broccoli for a few minutes, adding the garlic after 30 seconds. Next, add the chicken stock, cover with a lid and braise the broccoli for 2–3 minutes until the stems are cooked but still have a bite to them. (Test them by spearing with the point of a kitchen knife, or even cutting a 1cm slice.) Remove the broccoli to a serving plate, spoon over a couple of spoonfuls of the pan juices and the oyster sauce, and serve immediately.

* Some oriental suppliers sell a cheaper ersatz version of oyster sauce, which should be avoided. Go for the real oyster sauce – check the label carefully.

Chow mein noodles

SERVES 4

3 cloves garlic, peeled and crushed
1 × 2.5 cm piece fresh root ginger, peeled and grated
4 tbsp peanut oil
1 shallot, peeled and cut into large dice
1 small red chilli, deseeded and finely sliced
60g sugar snap peas
450g fat egg noodles, blanched and drained
120g fresh beansprouts
3 spring onions, cut diagonally into chunks
1 × 120g tin tiny shrimps, drained
3 tbsp kecup manis (sweet soy sauce)
2 tbsp light soy sauce

Method

In a hot wok, fry the garlic and ginger in the oil for 20 seconds, and after another 30 seconds add the shallot, chilli and sugar snap peas. Stirring well, add the noodles and cook on for 1 minute. Add the beansprouts and spring onions with the shrimps. Cook for 1 minute more, keeping the noodles from sticking to the wok, and then finally turn off the flame, pour on the kecup manis and light soy sauce. Serve on a warm plate and eat with chopsticks.

Whole sea bass baked in salt

SERVES 2

Burying a whole piece of fish (or meat) in salt to cook it is traditional in the south of Spain, and has an oriental equivalent in Chinese cuisine. Very simply, the joint is seasoned or marinated and then baked in a bed of salt; this is cracked open, and the flesh is brushed free of salt before serving.

Nick first had a whole cod cooked this way in Jerez in the early 1980s and found it memorable. Here, for the purposes of indulgence, we have specified a whole sea bass, one of our favourites, but you could use any whole firm-fleshed fish with a delicate flavour, such as John Dory or snapper.

You will need an earthenware chicken brick to cook this dish in.

1 fennel bulb, cored and finely sliced
2 fresh bay leaves
a pinch of aniseed
juice of 1 lemon
1 whole sea bass, about 700–800g, gutted
1 tbsp olive oil
3 kg coarse Maldon sea salt

Method

Stuff the fennel slices, bay leaves, aniseed and lemon juice in the gut cavity of the fish. Smear the outside of the fish lightly with the olive oil and place in the chicken brick on a 2.5cm layer of salt. Pour in the remaining salt to cover the fish completely and then place in a preheated oven (180°C/350°C/gas mark 4) for 45–60 minutes (cooking times will vary with the size of the fish).

To serve, lift the fish clear of the salt (a salt crust will have formed around it). The skin should come away easily with the salt crust exposing the whole fish, perfectly cooked and seasoned.

Serve it with beansprouts and pak-choi or spinach wok-fried with a little soy sauce and sesame oil.

Prawn, ginger and spring onion dim sum, with a sweet and sour dip

170g fine pork mince
90g prawns, cooked and peeled
1 × 1cm piece fresh root ginger, peeled and
  finely chopped
3 spring onions, finely chopped
a pinch of freshly ground white pepper
½ tsp Maldon sea salt
1 tbsp soy sauce
20 wonton wrappers
peanut oil for deep-frying

SWEET AND SOUR SAUCE
1 tbsp cornflour
4 tbsp cold water
½ tbsp tomato purée
2 tbsp wine vinegar
2 tbsp orange juice
2 tbsp pineapple juice
2 tsp light soy sauce
2 tsp caster sugar
1 tbsp honey

Dim sum method

Place the pork, prawns, ginger, spring onion, seasonings and soy sauce in a bowl and beat together until well blended.

To assemble, simply place 2 tsp of the mixture in a wonton wrapper, gather up the corners, and twist the top closed.

Deep-fry in the oil (at 180°C/350°F) for a couple of minutes until done and then drain very well on paper towels. Keep warm for serving.

Sweet and sour dip method

Blend the cornflour with the water and then place in a pan with all the other ingredients. Simmer together for at least 4 minutes until the sauce has thickened and has a syrupy texture.

Pork, shrimp and water chestnut dim sum

450g plain flour
175ml boiling water
175ml cold water
450g finely minced pork
140g prawns, cooked, peeled and minced
2 tbsp finely chopped spring onion
2 tbsp finely grated fresh root ginger
1 tbsp light soy sauce
1½ tsp salt
a pinch of freshly ground black pepper
60g Chinese water chestnuts, finely chopped
1 bunch watercress, coarsely chopped
5½ tbsp peanut oil

TO SERVE
1 recipe sweet chilli jam (see page 114)

Method

Place the flour in a bowl and make a well in the centre. Slowly add the boiling water, beating well to incorporate. When smooth, leave to rest for a few minutes, then add the cold water and knead well in a mixer with a dough hook.

Mix the pork, prawns, spring onion, ginger, soy sauce, and seasonings together. Add the water chestnuts and watercress and 1 tbsp of the peanut oil and blend well together.

Roll the dough into a long sausage shape, 4cm thick. Divide into 3cm lengths, and roll flat into small pancake shapes. Place 1 tbsp of the stuffing on the middle of each pancake and fold the halves of the dough together, wetting the edges and pinching them to make sure they stick *tight*. (No leakage when they're frying.)

Heat the remaining oil in a wok and fry the pancakes on a high heat for 2–3 minutes to brown the sides, then add 90ml water and cover. Steam the pancakes until the water has almost evaporated, then lower the heat and cook on until the water has completely evaporated.

Serve the dim sum with the brown side uppermost, with the sweet chilli jam.

Pacific Feast

GRILLED THAI PRAWNS

NAM PLA (FISH SAUCE)

PRAWN TOM YUM SOUP

STUFFED SQUIDS

STEAMED MUSSELS WITH LEMON GRASS,
CORIANDER AND LIME LEAVES

CRAB AND LOBSTER FISHCAKES
ON GREEN PAPAYA SALAD

Grilled Thai prawns

SERVES 4

16 large fresh tiger prawns for grilling

MARINADE
6 tbsp lime juice
4 large cloves garlic, peeled and crushed
4 small green chillies, deseeded and finely
  chopped
4 tsp palm sugar or jaggery (or use soft brown)
2 tsp tom yum paste (see page 136; or use
  chopped lemon grass, garlic and galangal)
1 × 400ml tin coconut milk
6 tbsp Thai fish sauce
6 tbsp light soy sauce
1 × 5cm piece of fresh root ginger, grated
6 kaffir lime leaves, finely chopped
a generous handful of chopped coriander
  (leaves and stalks)

TO SERVE
home-made nam pla

Method

Tiger prawns can be bought either head on or head off – in either case, take care to remove the black vein that runs down the spine.

Mix all the marinade ingredients together and leave the prawns in this for at least 1–2 hours. (You can also add flavour by injecting the prawns with fish sauce via a hypodermic syringe and needle. This gets the flavour right into the flesh!)

Brush the grill with oil to prevent the prawns sticking. Spear one or more on a soaked wooden skewer, lengthways. Grill over a high heat for about 3–4 minutes, depending on size. Do not overcook. Dip into the nam pla, and eat.

Nam pla (fish sauce)

60ml peanut oil
12 shallots (Thai red shallots if possible)
2 large cloves garlic, peeled and finely chopped
4 small red chillies, deseeded and finely chopped
4 tbsp Thai fish sauce
4 tbsp palm sugar or jaggery
4 tbsp lime juice
4 tbsp chicken stock (see page 57)

Method

Heat the oil in a small pan and fry the shallots and garlic until crisp and brown. Remove with a slotted spoon and reserve.

Pour off most of the oil, leaving a light

film on the pan, and return half of the cooked shallots and garlic to it. Then add the chillies, fish sauce, sugar, lime juice and stock and stir over a low heat until the mixture gets syrupy and all the sugar has melted. Then add the reserved shallots and garlic. Remove from the heat and use as a warm dip for the prawns.

Prawn tom yum soup

SERVES 8

1.1 litres chicken stock (see page 57)
2 tom yum stock cubes or paste*
120g small button mushrooms, thinly sliced
1 × 2.5cm piece of fresh root ginger, peeled, sliced wafer-thin and cut into fine strips
16 large lime leaves, washed
4 long lemon grass stalks, coarse outer layers peeled, chopped into small chips
32 raw king prawns, peeled and sliced in half lengthways
8 spring onions, roughly chopped
2 small red chillies, deseeded and chopped into fine rounds
juice of 1 lime

TO SERVE
a small handful of coriander leaves (no stems), chopped

Method

In a large saucepan, bring the stock to the boil, then reduce to a very slow simmer and crumble in and dissolve the tom yum cubes or paste. Add the mushrooms, ginger, lime leaves and lemon grass. Next add the prawns with the spring onions, chillies and lime juice; 1 minute will be enough to cook the prawns. Turn off the heat, and ladle the soup into bowls. To serve, simply sprinkle a few pinches of coriander onto the soup.

Tip Thai tom yum soup is quite fierce, being a hot-and-sour combination, so reduce the amount of chillies to make it milder.

* Tom yum paste cubes (or 'nam prik pow') can be obtained from oriental supermarkets. If supplies are difficult to find you can make your own up according to the following method on page 136.

Tom yum paste

3 tbsp finely chopped fresh garlic
4 tbsp peanut oil
4 tbsp finely chopped shallots
3 tbsp deseeded and roughly chopped dried
   red chilli
1 tbsp dried shrimp
1 tbsp Thai fish sauce
2 tsp palm sugar or jaggery

Method

In a small frying pan, fry the garlic in the peanut oil over a medium heat until golden brown. Remove, drain and reserve. Add the shallots to the oil and repeat, and do the same with the chillies.

In a processor, blitz the dried shrimp to a powder, then add the chillies, garlic and shallots and continue to blend all together. Add the fish sauce, blitz for a few seconds, then add the sugar and repeat. The mix should be a thick sauce, slightly oily, not actually a paste. It can be kept for 3 weeks in jars in the fridge, covered with a small layer of oil to seal (like pesto). As this is very fierce, use sparingly and taste your soups as you go!

Stuffed squids

SERVES 4

8 medium or 12 small squid, cleaned, heads
   retained★
1 small yellow onion or 2 shallots, peeled and
   chopped
8 tbsp olive oil
120g minced lean pork
3 large cloves garlic, peeled
2 small red chillies, deseeded and finely
   chopped
1 × 2.5cm peeled piece of fresh root ginger,
   grated
6 spring onions
120g prawns, peeled

2 tbsp Thai fish sauce
4 tbsp chopped coriander leaves
Maldon sea salt and freshly ground black pepper
1 tsp tomato purée

TO SERVE
lime wedges

Method

Trim off the squid wings, the easily removed flaps of fins along the side of the body, and chop them finely.

Fry the onions or shallots in a pan with half the olive oil and then add the pork, garlic, chillies and ginger and sauté for 10 minutes. Add the chopped squid and sauté for another 2 minutes. Fold in the remaining ingredients and season to taste.

Stuff the squid cavities with the mixture (not too tightly) and keep the flaps closed with soaked wooden toothpicks.

Brush with the remainder of the oil and chargrill on a very hot heat for about 5 minutes each side.

Serve with the lime wedges to squeeze and a sprinkling of sea salt.

★To clean squid, first take off the outer purply/pink skin and discard it. Now gut the squid, cut off the head above the eyes but retain the tentacles. Remove the clear 'plastic' inner bone (actually cartilage) and wash the body free of grit.

Steamed mussels with lemon grass, coriander and lime leaves

SERVES 8

3 kg mussels★
2 tbsp peanut oil
4 lemon grass stalks, peeled and cut on the diagonal into small chunks
6 large kaffir lime leaves
8 spring onions, chopped
1 small red chilli, deseeded and finely chopped
1 × 200 ml tin coconut milk
a large handful of coriander leaves

Method

Clean and debeard all the mussels and scrub them in fresh brine, discarding any broken ones and any that are open and don't close when tapped briskly.

Place a large saucepan on a high flame and in it pile the mussels with the peanut oil, lemon grass, lime leaves, spring onions and chilli. Cover with the lid. In a few minutes the mussels will sizzle and open their shells, releasing the juices within, which will help steam open the remainder. As the quantity is quite large you may have to use two pots or cook them in two batches.

When almost all the shells are open, stir the mussels around and discard any closed ones. Add the coconut milk and coriander leaves and stir through the mussels. To serve, spoon into bowls and ladle the spicy sauce over them. Provide clean bowls for the empty shells and some good bread to soak up the wonderful sauce.

★We favour large mussels (the bigger they are, the better they are). Often, regional varieties like the Welsh mussels can be quite small, although flavoursome. A trick is to place the mussels before cleaning into a large bucket or bin of brine (about 6 large handfuls of table salt to every 9 litres of cold tap water). Left over-night at room temperature the mussels will start to filter feed and thus clean themselves. If you swirl a handful of plain flour or fine ground oatmeal into the water they will feed and become fatter. This is not a process that can be continued indefinitely but is a useful way to refresh shellfish that may have come from far away and may have lost moisture or become starved en route.

Crab and lobster fishcakes on green papaya salad

SERVES 4

120g cooked lobster meat, chopped
150g cooked crabmeat (white/dark flesh mixed is fine)
150g cooked mashed potato (no cream or butter)
30g unsalted butter, melted
1 egg, beaten
1 tbsp chopped coriander
1 tbsp anchovy essence (Lea and Perrins)
dry white breadcrumbs for coating
8 tbsp coconut oil
Maldon sea salt and freshly ground black pepper

TO SERVE
1 recipe green papaya salad (see page 139)

Method

Mix the lobster, crab and potato well together, keeping the flakes coarse to retain some texture. Add a little of the melted butter to bind (use a little of the beaten egg, if necessary), stir in the coriander and season with the anchovy essence. Cool then form into 8 flat cakes 2.5cm thick. Dip into the beaten egg and then into the breadcrumbs to coat, then chill in a cool fridge for 1 hour.

To cook, simply heat the coconut oil until a cube of bread dropped in sizzles. Fry the fishcakes in the coconut oil for a few minutes until brown on both sides.

Serve on the papaya salad.

Green papaya salad

½ head Chinese leaves, chopped

90g carrots, peeled and coarsely grated

2 tbsp roughly ground roasted peanuts

2 small cloves garlic, peeled and chopped

350g firm but ripe papaya, peeled, deseeded and coarsely grated

150g cucumber, coarsely grated

2 tbsp dried shrimp, crumbled

2 small red fresh chillies, deseeded and chopped

2 tomatoes, skinned and sliced

2 tbsp palm sugar

4 tbsp chopped fresh mint leaves

4 tbsp chopped fresh coriander leaves

4 tbsp Thai fish sauce

4 tbsp lime juice

Method

Spread chopped Chinese leaves on each plate as a base.

Combine all the salad ingredients, starting with the hardest, and then add the liquids. Mix gently – don't mush together. The strong liquid draws juices from the salad materials so don't prepare until the very last minute.

BAKLAVA AND TURKISH COFFEE

PEACH ICE CREAM WITH BOURBON

ARMAGNAC PRUNES WITH SAUTERNES
CARAMEL CREAMS

BRANDIED APRICOT FILOS WITH
POWDERED CRYSTALLIZED ORANGE

HOT RASPBERRY SOUFFLÉ

NOSH PECAN FUDGE BROWNIES
WITH WHITE CHOCOLATE AND
SAMBUCA SAUCE

VANILLA ICE CREAM BAKED IN
MERINGUE, WITH A WARM MOCHA
SABAYON SAUCE

COCONUT AND WATER CHESTNUT
CUSTARD

PANETTONE PUDDING WITH COGNAC

RASPBERRY ICE CREAM WITH CASSIS

MANGO KULFI

Sweetly Indulgent

The debate about whether you should have dessert after or before the cheese rages on. We prefer to have the cheeses before, so you end up with a sweet taste in your mouth prior to coffee – or any other post-prandials! But it's up to you.

We have a confession to make. Although we have no aversion to sweet things, savoury is really our thing. A craving for some charcuterie is far more usual than any dreams of profiteroles. Having said that, there is something majestic about a rich pudding to round off the meal.

One shouldn't forget that not all desserts need cooking. Even on supermarket shelves there is now a huge selection of exotic fruits which make for a special array of colours and tastes, from horned melons to baby coconuts, so treat yourselves at any time – just ensure that the fruits are ready for eating. There's nothing worse than hard peaches: we'd rather eat a cricket ball!

Also, don't ignore the Chocolate Factor. Whether your tastes run to white, dark, milk, liqueur or plain, you can please most people with an array of sumptuous discs of Swiss or Belgian chocolates.

If you've got any room left, you can still go for seconds of the main course.

Baklava and Turkish coffee

SERVES 10

Baklava is actually a generic name for the many different styles of pastries that we associate with the Middle East. However, it is this archetypal diamond-cut shape flaky filo that most of us would call 'baklava' when feasting with panthers at the local Greek restaurant or Lebanese coffee house.

This is surprisingly easy to make, and being fairly syrupy will keep in a cool sealed tin for some days without going stale. We have specified fresh filo pastry here: frozen will do, but we think it's always best to hang on for this one until fresh is available; it really makes all the difference between an OK result and a truly memorable one, especially for your Ottoman Feast (page 115)!

SYRUP
350g caster sugar
2 tbsp thick strong honey (Greek Mountain is good)
250ml water
2 tbsp lemon juice
3 tbsp orange-blossom water

PASTRY
450g fresh filo pastry
170g unsalted butter, melted
250g pistachios, shelled and finely chopped★

Method

Make the syrup by dissolving the sugar, honey, water and lemon juice in a medium saucepan on a simmer until thick and syrupy. Add the orange-blossom water and allow to cool, then refrigerate for 1 hour.

Cut the filo sheets to fit a bakewell pan or baking tray (one with 3–4cm high sides). The baklava should be about 2cm high, finally.

Brush the sides and base of the tray with some of the butter. Lay half of the trimmed filo sheets onto the baking tray, one after the other, using a pastry brush to butter each sheet. Next spread the chopped pistachios over the filo, and pour 5 tbsp of the prepared syrup over evenly. Cover with the remaining filo sheets and brush each layer with melted butter as before. Finish the top layer with melted butter and then, using a very sharp knife, cut the whole tray into diamond-shaped sections, cutting evenly to the base of the filo layer.

Now bake for 45 minutes in a pre-heated oven (160°C/325°F/gas mark 3), then increase the temperature to 200°C/400°F/gas mark 6 for another 15 minutes to brown up the top and help the dessert rise slightly.

Finally, on removing from the oven, pour over the remaining cold syrup and leave the whole tray to cool. Score through each shape before serving to ensure a clean lift from the tray and serve with strong black coffee.

* You can do this in a blender on pulse.

Turkish coffee

We have tried this drink both with and without sugar, and it doesn't seem to work well without it, although we have reduced the sugar level here to a point more suitable for a European palate. Turks would probably have double the amount we have specified. Be careful not to swig the muddy bit at the bottom.

Brits call this style of making and serving coffee Turkish, although it is much the same as doing it Greek, Cypriot or Lebanese style. Describe it as Turkish to someone of Armenian descent, however, and you'll get some very dark looks. The point is that the simmer-in-the-jug method is Ottoman in origin and everyone in the Middle East has their own way of doing it. It is imperative to use a proper bean (Arabian Mocha Java is the recommended blend), well roasted and ground extra-fine to a powdery, icing-sugar appearance. Like the fine grind of the espresso mix, it needs these properties to release the essences in the correct fashion.

To do this strictly by the book, you will need a long-handled coffee jug (called an *ibrik*) with a flat base to boil the water in. Some are of elaborately engraved brass or copper but modern efforts can be aluminium or steel. Most come in two sizes – enough for two people or a larger size that will serve about six. However, if you have to, improvise with a straight-sided saucepan. Most coffee is drunk as a strong short beverage and the grounds will need a minute to settle at the bottom of the cup, so this is not a drink for a quick caffeine blast like an espresso – it should be sipped and lingered over after a good dinner, and refills should be endlessly forthcoming. Mick recently had a coffee in this style after dinner with Ma and Pa Nosh in a Lebanese coffee house on the Edgware Road in London – famous as 'Little Beirut', the centre for most of the West End Arab population. Staying a reasonably lazy fifty minutes (enough for a few baklavas and a respectable number of refills), he went to pay the bill. The owner was most perturbed and asked whether something was wrong. On being assured that 'Everything was fine, it is just time we were on our way,' he looked relieved and explained that in their country patrons would be expected to stay for between an hour and a half to three hours after dinner, depending on the degree of haste they were in. Relative Nosh hastiness had made him worried that all wasn't up to expectations with his coffee!

The Lebanese have a particular fondness for adding flavours to their coffee, such as a few ground cardamom seeds, but this is an acquired taste.

PER PERSON/DEMITASSE CUP
2 tbsp finely ground Turkish coffee
1 tsp caster sugar
90 ml filtered cold water

Stir the coffee and sugar into the water in the jug and place on a high heat to bring to the boil. Watch the jug, and as the water starts to boil, remove it from the heat until the froth subsides. Reduce the flame to a simmer, and replace the jug for a few minutes to let it froth up again. This process should be repeated three times, taking care not to let the coffee boil over. Then it should be left to rest for 2–3 minutes (to let the grounds settle) before pouring.

Pouring should be done slowly and carefully in order not to disturb the grounds. Once in the cup, the coffee should be left for 1 minute for the grounds to settle to the bottom of the cup and then it is ready for drinking.

Peach ice cream with bourbon

SERVES 8

Use ripe, flawless fruit. Peaches at peak of condition will have a full aroma, and some give to their surface.

The addition of liquor gives this a sophisticated taste, but it retains the simple texture of a granita fruit dessert. If you like it extra-sweet, use Southern Comfort.

Nectarines would be a good substitute.

8 ripe medium peaches (about 450g weight
of peeled, stoned and chopped fruit)
120g caster sugar* (or to taste)
150 ml bourbon (rye) whiskey (Wild Turkey,
Jim Beam or Jack Daniel's)
1.2 litres double cream
¾ tsp vanilla essence

Method

In a mixing bowl stir the sugar into the bourbon until dissolved, then tip in the peaches and mash with a potato masher until everything is of an even texture. (You could use a blender, but this manual method is good for a nice coarse texture.) Whip the cream until just thickened, not too stiff, and add the vanilla essence. Fold this into the peach mixture and mix thoroughly.

Pour into a plastic container and freeze for 24 hours. There is no need to stir at any time.

This ice cream has a very simple home-made feel to it, the fruit water in it forming slightly crunchy icy crystals. It will scoop better if the tub is left for 10 minutes at room temperature to thaw slightly.

* Pale Muscovado sugar tastes great in this recipe but gives it an unusual brownish tinge that may not be all that appetizing.

Armagnac prunes with Sauternes caramel creams

SERVES 8

750g Californian prunes
1 glass armagnac
150 ml pear juice
juice of 1 lemon
50g caster sugar

CRÈME CARAMEL
240g granulated sugar
225 ml water
100 ml Sauternes (dessert wine)
6 eggs
90g caster sugar
2 vanilla pods, split
625 ml milk
pinch of salt

Prunes method

Choose the 'moist'-style of ready-to-eat prunes such as Sunsweet, which come already de-stoned. (If you cannot get these, take out the stones by making a slit along one side with a sharp knife and removing the pits while trying not to destroy the overall shape of the fruits.)

Soak the fruits in the armagnac, preferably overnight, or for at least a few hours. Drain, reserving any armagnac for the sauce. Simmer them in the pear and lemon juices with the sugar, stirring lightly to dissolve the sugar. About 15 minutes' slow simmering should be enough. Remove the prunes and set aside. The sauce can then be reduced by boiling to a thick syrup. Pour over the prunes and keep in a cool place.

Crème caramel method

Make the caramel first. Stir the granulated sugar and the water in a pan on a high heat for 8–12 minutes or so until golden brown. Do not allow the colour to advance too much, as the caramel will cook on after it has been removed from the heat. Pour immediately into individual ramekin-style soufflé dishes, where it will cool and harden. Reduce the wine in a saucepan on a medium high heat to about a quarter of its volume, and set aside.

Now make the custard by whisking the eggs and caster sugar together until the sugar has dissolved. Add the vanilla pods to the milk, bring to the boil, and take it off the heat immediately. Add the salt. Next, add the reduced wine and whisk into the eggs, blending it quickly and thoroughly. Strain the resulting mix through a fine sieve to remove any stray egg strands and pour into the ramekins. Stand in a bain-marie filled with enough boiling water to come to two-thirds of the way up the dishes and cover each ramekin with foil. Bake in a preheated oven (180°C/ 350°F/ gas mark 4) for 40 minutes or so, testing the setting point of a sample dish by tapping and gently shaking it to see if it's set. When you are convinced that the crème caramels are no longer in a fluid state, remove them from the oven, cool, then chill in a cold fridge. To serve, turn the puddings out onto individual plates and arrange the armagnac prunes alongside.

Brandied apricot filos with powdered crystallized orange

MAKES 20 'PARCELS'

We have to thank Mother M. Nosh and Marie Hekimian for the winning elements in this delicate sweetmeat. At a charity appeal for an Armenian earthquake fund, these pastries were selling, literally, like hot cakes, and helped to raise hundreds of dollars. Each batch went up in price, setting a kind of Dow-Jones index for desserts!

Fresh apricots are only around for a short season, so snap them up when available. It is worth noting that of all the fruits there are two in particular which do not ripen after picking – pineapples and apricots. Get your fruit off the tree if possible. If you run into someone who grows apricots, make friends and beg off them all you can.

Drained tinned ones will do, but like all tinned goods they have a low flavour quotient and tend to be too mushy. Better to use the packets of stoned, moist-style semi-dried fruits – which will at least have a dense enough texture. The powdered crystallized orange peel is for extra indulgence. It is simply peel that is twice boiled in sugar syrup (once would make marmalade) and dried in between until hard and brittle then powdered in a grinder to create a highly flavoured orange dusting powder that is a whole dimension above

simple icing sugar. As it keeps for many months in a tightly sealed airtight plastic container, you can make a fair quantity and keep it for future use. Seville oranges are particularly good for this.

CRYSTALLIZED ORANGE PEEL
3 organic or unwaxed oranges
180g caster sugar
400ml water

FILO PARCELS
10 fresh ripe apricots, stoned and halved (or 20 preserved halves)
4 tbsp brandy
1 packet fresh filo pastry
175g unsalted butter, melted

Peel method

You will need to start 3 or 4 days in advance. Peel just the skin of the washed, dried orange with a potato peeler (skin only, no white pith). Boil this in a syrup made from half the sugar and half the water for 5 minutes and then dry off on a wire rack for 4 hours. Then boil again in a fresh syrup made with the remaining sugar and water and dry again on the wire rack until brittle, about 48 hours. (We also tried using a fan oven set on the lowest setting with the door slightly ajar to allow free passage of air and the peel dried in under 8 hours.) Grind in a clean coffee grinder and store in a sealed airtight plastic container.

Filo method

Soak the apricot halves in the brandy overnight. Prepare the filo by cutting it into long strips about 7.5cm × 2cm. Paint each strip of filo with melted butter, and place an apricot half at one end. Fold up into little triangular parcels, rather like a samosa shape, until you have 4 or 5 layers encasing the apricot. It's easiest to roll the triangles up across the entire width of the packet-made length of the filo and then cut away the extra 2–3cm. Paint a final dollop of melted butter on top, and bake the parcels in a preheated oven on a floured baking tray for 12–15 minutes at 205°C/400°F/gas mark 6 until a light golden-brown colour. Using a palette knife or slice, lift the parcels carefully onto a wire rack to let them cool slightly. Dust liberally with the powdered orange peel. Best eaten while still warm – perfect with after-dinner coffee. They will keep, but after some hours tend to get moist and soggy from the filling.

Hot raspberry soufflé

SERVES 8

Soufflés seem like hard work, but really they are quite easy once you have the mixture and oven temperatures right You'll need individual ramekin-type soufflé dishes for this one.

a little unsalted butter, melted
635g caster sugar
8 Amaretti biscuits (Di Saronno)
1.2kg fresh raspberries
1.25 litres water
1 tbsp lemon juice
675ml milk
90g plain flour
60g unsalted butter

3 tbsp framboise liqueur
8 egg whites

Method

Prepare each soufflé dish first. Brush the inside surfaces with melted butter and sprinkle 1 tsp or so of sugar into each one. Rotate it so that all the inside surfaces are covered. Get rid of any excess sugar. Place the dishes on a baking sheet, and put a biscuit in each, plus a few raspberries.

Make a little purée with most of the remaining raspberries (you want some whole for the middle of the soufflés), 375g of the sugar and the water, bringing it slowly to the boil to melt the sugar, then boiling to reduce for 5 minutes. Whizz in the blender and rub through a sieve to remove the pips.

Return about two-thirds of the purée to the pan and simmer to reduce it to a jam consistency. Set aside. Add the lemon juice to the remaining purée and keep warm (this will be the sauce).

Preheat the oven to 220°C/425°F/gas mark 7.

Next, combine the milk and 150g of the sugar in a saucepan. Bring slowly to the boil to melt the sugar then add another 90g sugar. Beat together with a stout whisk. Stir in the flour, beat until smooth, and pour on the boiling milk, whisking all the time, off the heat, to create a cream sauce.

Return to the heat and boil for about 3–4 minutes, then flake in most of the butter and keep warm. Dot the rest of the butter over the surface to prevent a skin forming.

To assemble, simply fold the raspberry 'jam' into the custard, along with the framboise liqueur. Beat the egg whites until stiff and forming soft peaks, then mix a third of them together with the custard, before folding the rest in carefully, in two batches, to prevent the air being lost from the mixture.

Half-fill the prepared dishes with the mixture, then place some fresh raspberries on top. Cover with some more mixture. Flatten the surface lightly with a wetted palette knife, and bake in the preheated oven for 7–10 minutes until well risen. Serve with the warm raspberry sauce.

Nosh pecan fudge brownies with white chocolate and Sambuca sauce

SERVES 8

We certainly can't take credit for inventing what must be the ultimate American cake-cum-cookie, sticky and rich, served cut up into squares. However, in our usual devil-may-care style we have transformed this popular snack into a fully-fledged dessert for chocoholics everywhere with the addition of a hot white-chocolate sauce with liqueur – an indulgence of the finest ingredients.

Some brownie recipes call for a more 'cakey' type of approach, but in our view that defeats the whole point of getting that chewy, fudgy, moist texture.

White chocolate, although tasty to nibble, spells death to the taste buds in

cooking. This is because it has none of that crucial dark cocoa mass. We wanted both texture and flavour, though, so it's in there, but Noshed up in flavour terms with Sambuca. The liqueur lends some of its strength to the sauce, too.

240g unsalted butter
150g top-quality plain bitter chocolate, broken into pieces
90g semi-sweet plain chocolate (Bourneville will do), broken into pieces
400g caster sugar
4 medium eggs
180g plain flour, sifted
2 tsp vanilla essence
180g coarsely chopped pecans

TOPPING
120g soft brown sugar
3 tbsp unsalted butter, softened
150ml single cream
½ tsp vanilla essence
180g pecans, medium to finely chopped

SAUCE
240g good quality white chocolate, melted
60ml single cream
60ml Sambuca

Cake method

Preheat the oven to 180°C/350°F/gas mark 4. Using extra butter and flour, lightly grease and dust a 30 × 23cm tin.

Melt the butter and the two chocolates together over a low heat, stirring until melted and smooth. Allow to cool slightly.

Beat the sugar into the eggs until frothy (add the sugar slowly), until the mixture is thick and pale coloured. Stir in the chocolate/butter mixture and blend together well. Stir in the flour and mix, then add the vanilla essence and pecans.

Spread into the prepared baking tin and bake in the preheated oven for about 20 minutes. Do not overbake or the brownies will taste bitter and dry. Insert a fine metal prong to see if it comes away clean: if there is a slight stickiness on the prong, don't worry; the latent heat that is within the cake will help to finish off the baking process.

Topping method

While the cake is in the oven, melt the sugar with the butter in a small saucepan. Stir in the cream until well blended, then remove from the heat and add the vanilla essence and pecans.

Assembly

When the cake is done, rest it for 5 minutes then spread the topping over it and grill under a high heat for a few minutes to bubble the cream (don't let it burn). This creates a crisp, nutty tasting topping for the fudge brownie – and will give a truly fudgy, dense and moistened result.

The by now very sticky cake is left to

cool for 10 minutes or so before cutting into portions. Meanwhile you can make the ridiculously easy sauce by melting the white chocolate in the cream in a saucepan on a very low heat or over a pan of gently bubbling water. Add the Sambuca when fully melted. Serve while still warm to hot.

Vanilla ice cream baked in meringue, with a warm mocha sabayon sauce

SERVES 8

This is a kind of small Baked Alaska, a version for individual portions. The combination of crisp, chewy meringue and solid creamy interior guarantees requests for seconds – make up a few extra dishes in case!

1 recipe vanilla ice cream (as raspberry ice
  cream, page 156)
8 thin circles of sponge to fit the top of your
  ice-cream moulds

MERINGUE
4 egg whites
a pinch of salt
240g caster sugar

SABAYON SAUCE
8 egg yolks
120g caster sugar
180ml egg Marsala (Marsala all'Uovo)*
60ml Kahlua coffee liqueur
2 tbsp unsweetened cocoa powder

Ice cream method

Make a custard exactly as described on page 156, omitting the raspberries and liqueur, of course!

Meringue method

Only when the ice cream is frozen, and you are near to serving, do you make the meringue.

Whisk the egg whites with the salt to a stiff mix, then whisk in 3 tbsp of the sugar and continue whisking until the mix is smooth and shiny. Fold in the remaining sugar with a metal spoon. Place the mix in a piping bag with a 1cm plain nozzle and twist the bag closed until ready for piping.

To bake the meringue, preheat the oven to 230°C/450°F/gas mark 8. Dip the plastic ice cream container into warm water for a minute or so to allow easy decanting of portions. Put a small thin disc of plain sponge underneath each ice-cream shape as a mat, so the ice will not melt against the baking tray's base. Then pipe the meringue mix around the ice cream in an ascending spiral coil to completely cover it. Bake in the oven for about 5 minutes. This will be enough to brown up high-spots on the meringue, but not to melt the central frozen core.

Mocha sauce method

Meanwhile, some very deft timing is called for. Start whisking the sauce the minute the meringue goes into the oven and it should all be ready for the finished result.

Place the egg yolks, the sugar and the liquids in a metal-based round-bottomed wok (cleaned and spotlessly grease-free), and using a metal balloon whisk stir the mixture vigorously. When consistent, move the wok over a medium flame – about 5cm from the tip. (Many books call for a bain-marie to avoid the indignity of curdling your sauce, but with some energy and a careful eye to keep the pan away from the fiercest part of the flame, you can cut down the time for this part.) About 4–6 minutes of vigorous whisking should be enough. The final consistency should be a rich velvety foamy sauce that will sit on the plate without spreading too far – but thin enough to flow around the ice cream meringue slightly.

Pour a dash of the mocha sabayon sauce around the meringue-encased ice cream and serve immediately.

* Marsala is a fortified dark wine from Sicily. Ensure it is the dark sweet 'egg' Marsala. Don't use the pale thin Tio Pepe sherry-like Marsala – it won't give the right result.

Coconut and water chestnut custard

SERVES 8

We first discovered this dessert in a North London Thai delicatessen, where the family who run it still make and sell home-made Thai food for takeaway. Although the proprietors were keen to *sell* the product, they were tight-lipped about its constituents and firmly resisted all attempts to giveaway the family secrets. This recipe has therefore had to be reconstructed on a trial and error basis, involving buying a considerable number of ready-made ones to test and try. The end result is a very delicate and creamy end to a spicy meal, and the water chestnut (the hardest bit to 'deconstruct') a delicious crunchy element to finish with.

You will need 8 large dessert ramekins, 7.5cm high.

unsalted butter for greasing, melted
300g caster sugar
500ml thick coconut milk
2 tsp rosewater
1 tsp fine salt
6 eggs, lightly beaten
2 × 120g cans Chinese water chestnuts,
  drained and finely chopped
ground pistachios for decoration

Method

Grease the ramekins with some melted butter. Mix the sugar and the coconut milk in a food processor. Add the rosewater and salt and blitz for a few seconds more. Add the eggs and mix together.

Place a 1cm layer of the water chestnut in the bottom of each ramekin, and gently pour in the custard mix. Steam on the top of a preheated steamer for about 30 minutes, or until set. Then sprinkle with the ground pistachios and leave to cool. When cool, refrigerate for 1 hour before serving.

It will keep 2 days in the fridge if covered.

Panettone pudding with cognac

This dessert can be served hot or even tepid, but loses its appeal when cooler. If you find you haven't had enough cholesterol, serve it with clotted cream.

300ml whole milk
6 tbsp vanilla sugar★
8 egg yolks
300ml single cream
zest of 1 orange and 2 lemons
1 tbsp cognac
160g unsalted butter, melted
1 large loaf of Italian panettone, sliced

Method

Make the custard first. Bring the milk to the boil, and dissolve in it 4 tbsp of the vanilla sugar. If you don't have vanilla sugar, use plain caster sugar with 2 tsp vanilla essence. Remove from the heat.

Whisk the egg yolks into the cream with the zest and the cognac, and add this mix to the boiled milk, whisking vigorously together.

Grease the inside surfaces of a large oval gratin dish (a cast-iron Le Creuset type is good) with some of the melted butter. Cut the panettone slices into small triangles, and dip one side of each lightly into the melted butter. Layer the triangles of buttered bread in rows to cover the dish – propping each one up against another so they are leaning slightly at an angle. (This will allow the custard mix to flow down between the layers and penetrate and cook evenly.) Now arrange another layer of butter-dipped cake the other way. Finish off with a third layer of panettone, arranged in the opposite direction. Pour the custard mix over slowly. Ensure each top piece is soaked, and rest the pudding for 15 minutes to allow the fluid to settle and penetrate the whole dish.

Then sprinkle with the last 2 tbsp of vanilla sugar and bake in a preheated oven (180°C/350°C/gas mark 4) for about 30 minutes. The top of the pudding should be golden brown, with the panettone quite crisp in parts, while the inner texture should be moist, soft and light, like a soufflé, but not runny. The position in the oven can be quite critical if you don't have a fan oven; if in doubt, move the dish up or down inside the oven accordingly.

* Vanilla sugar can easily be made at home by steeping 3 or 4 vanilla pods in a jam jar of caster sugar for a few weeks. Keep turning the mixture to let the essence of the vanilla permeate the crystals – useful here and in other custard recipes. Once used, just top up the jar with sugar and start again. The pods are good for a couple of years' use.

Raspberry ice cream with cassis

SERVES 8

The addition of cassis liqueur makes this properly rich and fruity. For this, we cast our minds back to the early 60s, and memories of ice cream long before the days of Magnums, Häagen-Dazs and Ben & Jerry's. All we had then was Cornish Vanilla, Neapolitan . . . and then came Raspberry Ripple! In this modern version the fruit is real, and properly integrated.

8 egg yolks
150g caster sugar
1 vanilla pod, split
750ml whole milk
250g raspberries
a dash of crème de cassis (de Dijon is best)
150ml double cream, lightly whipped

Method

For the vanilla ice cream custard base, whisk the egg yolks in a round bowl with half the sugar until the

mixture goes creamy and forms ribbons.

Squeeze the black paste – the seeds – from the vanilla pod, and place them in a saucepan with the remaining sugar, the vanilla pod and the milk and bring to the boil. When the milk has risen, pour it onto the sugar/yolk mix, whisking vigorously. Pour the mixture back into the saucepan and place it over a very low heat, stirring continuously, until the custard thickens enough to coat the back of a spoon. Do not let the mixture sit or overheat as it will boil and produce congealed 'scrambled egg' – so keep an eye on it as you whisk. When thickened, pass the custard through a fine conical strainer and let it cool completely. Place a layer of clingfilm on top to stop a skin forming. Wash and dry the vanilla pod – it can be used again.

Sort through the raspberries, let them dry and then blitz them in a processor with the crème de cassis. Add the cream and process for a few seconds. Then add to the custard and mix together thoroughly. Pour into a plastic container and place in the freezer. Keep covered, and stir every hour until it's fully frozen.

To serve, let the ice cream warm up at room temperature for 5 minutes to allow easy scooping of portions.

Mango kulfi

SERVES 8

This creamy tasting ice cream is in Nosh terms probably about the only decent Indian sweet. It would be good served as the finale to our Indian Feast (see page 96).

Despite its creamy flavour, it is made with milk that has been reduced. Traditional dishes call for cardamom-type flavourings but we have adapted a basic recipe to include mango, to build up the Nosh quotient nicely in flavour terms.

2.25 litres whole milk
2 ripe mangoes, peeled, stone removed, flesh puréed
6 tbsp caster sugar

15g blanched almonds (unsalted), chopped
30g unsalted pistachios, chopped

Method

Bring the milk to the boil in a heavy-based saucepan. When it has risen, turn the heat down and reduce it on a very slow simmer. Let it lose about two-thirds of its volume so that you end up with about 750ml. A milky skin will form on top as you simmer; just stir it in – no problem. This will take ages, up to an hour.

When the milk has reduced add the mango purée, sugar and almonds, and stir for another 5 minutes on a very low heat, then transfer the mixture to a large bowl and let it cool completely.

Add half the pistachios and stir them in. Cover the bowl with clingfilm and place it in the freezer. At the same time place 8 individual cups (empty small cream or yoghurt cartons make good moulds) into the freezer to chill. Stir the mix every 15 minutes or so, to break up any crystals that form, and repeat until the mix becomes firm and nearly impossible to stir.

Sprinkle a few pistachio gratings into each container then divide the mix between the containers. Cover each mould with film or foil and replace in the freezer compartment to finally harden. To serve, simply dip each mould in warm water for 10 seconds to melt the sides and invert onto a pudding dish. The nuts should top off this dessert nicely.

NOSH BLOODY MOSES

SWEET LASSI WITH PISTACHIOS

ICED KAHLUA COFFEE

BOLLINGER RD WITH CHILLED
WILD STRAWBERRIES

GIMLETS

Down the Hatch

Just as there's no smoke without fire, the Nosh philosophy of indulgence implies no eating without drinking. Here is a selection of drinks that we have enjoyed over the years – but feel free to concoct your own.

To accompany the meal, of course, you're most likely to want to indulge in a fine wine. Recommendations are highly temporal, depending on harvests, available vintages, and new developments. Find a good wine writer that you identify with (our favourites are Oz Clarke and Richard O'Neil) and stick to their seasonal recommendations – you're unlikely to go wrong. For the casual wine buyer Majestic Wine Warehouses always seem to have a superb selection and are very helpful with giving advice.

Don't ignore ports and dessert wines for extra lavishness, and seek out vintage armagnacs for a flavoursome change from cognacs. Vintage rums – long seen as a nautical preference for landlocked sailors and mad West Indians 'locked in' to a 'shebeen' – are also emerging with a more sophisticated image than yesteryear for the demanding drinker.

Nosh bloody Moses

SERVES 1–6 (DEPENDING ON THIRST)

It all started in the bar of the Beverly Hills Hotel, having just had a fabulous pasta and a great bottle of Napa Valley wine for lunch in the adjoining courtyard. What better after a memorable lunch than to go for the full session? So we decided to start with an excellent Bloody Mary, to cleanse the palate, so to speak. The Beverly Hills Hotel knows how to make a good one, but ours is even more over the top.

You know how British pubs just put a meagre shot of vodka in a glass, top it up with a tiny bottle of tomato juice and, if you're lucky, a shot of Worcester sauce? Big deal!

If that's all you know a Bloody Mary to be, then read on, because this may change your life, or at least will liven it up. What we're trying to achieve here is a complex yet flavoursome drink with a little heat. (It's most important not to *over*do the heat, as it will mask the many different flavours.)

The clam juice brings a whiff of the sea to the proceedings, and biblical Moses was a dab hand with the sea, so we named it after him.

This manna may give you – or cure – a hangover!

1 × 300 ml can premium tomato juice
1 litre jar Clamato clam juice

juice of ½ a lemon
juice of 1 lime
½ tsp finely ground black pepper
½ tsp celery salt
3 shakes Tabasco sauce (or to taste –
*   remember, not too much heat)*
6 shakes Worcestershire sauce
2 tbsp horseradish (if mild, 1 only if strong)
*   or a pinch of wasabe powder (Japanese*
*   horseradish mustard)*
ice cubes
good-quality vodka to taste (e.g. Absolut or
*   Finlandia)*

TO SERVE
celery sticks

Method

In a large jug, mix the juices and seasonings together. Check for saltiness (some brands of juice are quite highly salted, others very plain). Place ice cubes into a large tumbler and pour over a good measure of vodka: about 2 pub measures, 30–60ml, should do it, but add more if you want more fun! Top up with the juice mixture and stir around gently, with a fresh cut crisp stick of celery . . . instant Bloody Moses!

Sweet lassi with pistachios

SERVES 2

Many wine pundits have deliberated long and hard about the best wine to go with curry. So far, we have yet to be convinced that any wine is suitable. Wine is generally a delicately flavoured item, and hardly complements such strong, spicy food. Ice-cold lager scores far higher on the Noshometer. Lassi's a good alternative; a smooth-yet-sourish flavour does not fight the heat but, gently sipped, soothes the palate. One type of lassi uses salt, but in our opinion it doesn't pass muster.

600 ml whole milk
6 tbsp full-fat plain 'sour' yoghurt★
2 tbsp caster sugar
4 ice cubes
a pinch of salt
2 aniseeds

TO SERVE
2 ice cubes
1 tbsp ground pistachios

Method

Put all the ingredients into a blender and whizz on fast speed for 30 seconds. Decant into two silver beakers (or chilled long glasses) and float an ice cube in each. A pinch of ground pistachios completes the dish.

★ There are a number of yoghurt brands that pride themselves on their mildness, particularly the German-made brands. While these are fine in other uses, we would recommend here a fully-loaded 'sour' type (even sheep's milk yoghurt would do).

Iced Kahlua coffee

Iced coffee is fab to refresh you on a hot summer's day. The addition of Kahlua expands the taste dimension and ensures a lavish effect.

PER PERSON
3 tbsp Kahlua (Mexican coffee liqueur)
ice cubes (made with frozen coffee, if desired)

300 ml strong dark-roast coffee (brewed triple strength with some ice cubes added to cool it to room temperature)
1 tbsp whipped cream
grated plain chocolate for topping

Method

Pour the Kahlua into a jug, over the rocks. Pour cold coffee into the mixture, float the cream over and grate on the chocolate.

Bollinger RD with chilled wild strawberries

SERVES 1 (NOSH)

Wild strawberries can be found in areas of woods that do not have too many ramblers going through them. A favourite location is disused railway tracks. They are hard and chewy but have an incomparable flavour. If you don't have a particularly good local disused railway or fruiterer, Panzers of St John's Wood, London, have good supplies. For champagne, Bollinger is our current favourite but any fine Grand Marque champagne will do. Ensure you get the Brut, extra-dry version. RD stands for Récemment Dégorge, or 'recently disgorged'. This doesn't mean what you might think. Actually, the wine has stood on the yeast lees for longer than normal, to impart more depth of flavour and general complexity to the finished product. Having a longer lying time it has the 'reserve' quality befitting a premium label.

1 bottle Bollinger RD, chilled to 2°C
3 dozen wild strawberries, chilled to 1°C

Method

Rinse the wild strawberries in cold water, removing any chaff, dry carefully, and almost freeze them.

Floated in a chilled glass of champagne they will act as ice cubes and can be a delicious last bite on the palate when the glass is drained fully.

Gimlets

A gimlet is a small sharp boring tool used to bore holes or tap barrels – and eventually came to describe this small sharp drink. Someone we know used to steal this particular concoction as a child from their father's drinks cabinet! Father always kept a close eye on the tonic level but the lime juice was never scrutinized . . . and somehow the diminishing level of gin escaped his attention. Where there's a will, there's a way!

PER PERSON
2 measures gin (Tanqueray is good)
¾ measure Rose's Lime Cordial

1 measure cold soda water (if you require a long drink – but we don't recommend it)

TO SERVE
crushed ice
1 wedge of lime

Method

Shake the liquids together in a cocktail shaker, then strain into a glass with crushed ice. Garnish with a wedge of fresh lime. (You can make gimlets with rum, tequila or vodka.)

Conversion Tables

These are practical conversions for use in the kitchen. In this book, dry spoon measures are rounded or heaped, not level.

OVEN TEMPERATURES

CENTIGRADE	FAHRENHEIT	GAS MARK
110	225	¼
130	275	1
150	300	2
160	325	3
180	350	4
190	375	5
200	400	6
220	425	7
230	450	8
250	475	9

DRY MEASURE

METRIC	IMPERIAL	METRIC	IMPERIAL	METRIC	IMPERIAL	METRIC	IMPERIAL	METRIC	IMPERIAL
8g	¼oz	90g	3oz	200g	7oz	450g	16oz	1.5kg	3½lb
15	½	120	4	225	8	675	1½	2	4½
30	1	140	5	250	9	900	2	2.3	5
60	2	175	6	285	10	1000	2¼	4.5	10

AMERICAN LIQUID MEASURES

1 tbsp (US) = 3 tsp (US) = ½ fl oz (US) = 14.785ml
1 C (US) = 8 oz / 8 fl oz (US) = 16 tbsp (US) = 237ml
1 pint (US) = 16 fl oz (US) = 28.88 cu. in. = 0.473 litre
1 pint (UK) = 20 fl oz = 34.68 cu. in. = 0.568 litre

LIQUID MEASURE

METRIC	IMPERIAL		AMERICAN
5ml	–	1 tsp	1 tsp
10	–	2	2
20	–	1 tbsp	1½ tbsp
25	1 fl oz	1½	2½
50	2	3	¼C
75	3	4	⅓C (6 tbsp)
100	4	⅕ pint	½C (¼ pint)
150	5	¼	⅔C
175	6	–	¾C
200	7	–	Scant 1C
250	8	⅓	1C (½ pint)
300	10	½	1¼C
400	14	¾	1¾C
450	15	¾	–
500	16	–	2C (1 pint)
575	20	1	2½C
700	25	1¼ pints	3C
750	27	–	3½C
900	32	1⅔	4C
1 litre	35	1¾	4½C
1.1 litres	40	2	5C
1.5	50	2½	6¼C
1.75	60	3	7½C
2	72	3½	9C
2.25	84	4	10½C
9	320	16	40C

Index

Index

173

Acknowledgements

We would like to acknowledge the support, inspiration and help of the following, without whom this book would not have been possible.

Mother and Father M. Nosh, Mother and Father N. Nosh, Gill Best, Jack Cloake, Marie Hekimian, Anna Longaretti, Bruce Warwick, Kelvin Murray, Jim Sennwick, Helena Donahue, Wayne Grant (of Grant's Fish Shop in Abbey Road, for fine supplies of fish and shellfish), Torz and Macatonia, and Macken's of Chiswick.

Gordon Wise and the Macmillan team – Sarah Bennie, Helen Surman, Wilf Dickie, Kate Judd, Neil Lang, Susan Fleming, Nicholas Blake, Liz Davis, Ann Cooke, and Morven Knowles.

Anthony Blackburn, John Sachs, George Allan Homegrown of Covent Garden, suppliers to the Nosh Brothers of top-quality fruit and vegetables, and British Meat for their supplies of fine quality meat.

About the Authors

Mick and Nick Nosh started their business collaboration in 1992, becoming renowned for their celebrity parties, after both had enjoyed extensive careers in the media, music and entertainment industries, and apprenticeships in kitchens around the world. Unable to find a restaurant in London to serve them the type of food they wanted to eat, in the surroundings in which they wanted to eat, the food served as they wanted it to be served, they opened their own in London's Fulham Road in 1993. Their reputation for great entertaining and superb, honest 'food with attitude' rapidly grew, and won wide critical acclaim. Following on from their Talk Radio food and drink programme and many other magazine, television and radio appearances, their barbecuing TV series, *Red Hot & Smokin'*, has appeared on the Carlton Food Network, followed by a series on seasonal foods, *Winter Nosh*. Their series *Save Your Bacon* for ITV was followed by a humorous look at the wealth of traditional Spanish food still to be found in Andalucia on the south coast of Spain, *Costa del Nosh*, again for Carlton Food Network. Mick and Nick have just returned from the far north of Scandinavia, capturing the essence of Viking Feasts for CFN's *Nordic Nosh*.